also by the editors at america's test kitchen

The Complete Slow Cooker

The Complete Make-Ahead Cookbook

The Complete Mediterranean Cookbook

The Complete Vegetarian Cookbook

The Complete Cooking for Two Cookbook

What Good Cooks Know

Cook's Science

The Science of Good Cooking

The Perfect Cookie

Bread Illustrated

Master of the Grill

Kitchen Smarts

Kitchen Hacks

100 Recipes: The Absolute Best Ways to Make the True Essentials

The New Family Cookbook

The America's Test Kitchen Cooking School Cookbook

The Cook's Illustrated Meat Book

The Cook's Illustrated Baking Book

The Cook's Illustrated Cookbook

The New Best Recipe

Soups, Stews, and Chilis

The America's Test Kitchen Quick Family Cookbook

The America's Test Kitchen Healthy Family Cookbook

The America's Test Kitchen Family Baking Book

The Best of America's Test Kitchen (2007–2018 Editions)

The Complete America's Test Kitchen TV Show Cookbook 2001–2018

Food Processor Perfection

Pressure Cooker Perfection

Vegan for Everybody

Naturally Sweet

Foolproof Preserving

Paleo Perfected

The How Can It Be Gluten-Free Cookbook: Volume 2

The How Can It Be Gluten-Free Cookbook

The Best Mexican Recipes

Slow Cooker Revolution Volume 2: The Easy-Prep Edition

Slow Cooker Revolution

The Six-Ingredient Solution

The America's Test Kitchen D.I.Y. Cookbook

Pasta Revolution

the cook's illustrated all-time best series

All-Time Best Sunday Suppers

All-Time Best Soups

All-Time Best Appetizers

cook's country titles

One-Pan Wonders

Cook It in Cast Iron

Cook's Country Eats Local

The Complete Cook's Country TV Show Cookbook

for a full listing of all our books

CooksIllustrated.com

AmericasTestKitchen.com

holiday
entertaining

holiday entertaining

the editors at
america's test kitchen

Library of Congress
Cataloging-in-Publication Data

Names:
   America's Test Kitchen (Firm), author.
Title: All time best holiday
   entertaining / by the editors at
   America's Test Kitchen
Other titles: Holiday entertaining
Description: Boston, MA : America's Test Kitchen, [2017] |
   Includes index.
Identifiers: LCCN 2017000742 | ISBN 9781940352992
Subjects: LCSH: Holiday cooking. |
   Entertaining. | LCGFT: Cookbooks.
Classification: LCC TX739 .A344 2017 | DDC 641.5/68--dc23
LC record available at
   https://lccn.loc.gov/2017000742

AMERICA'S TEST KITCHEN
21 Drydock, Suite 210E, Boston, MA 02210

Manufactured in China

10 9 8 7 6 5 4 3 2 1

Distributed by Penguin Random House Publisher Services
Tel: 800.733.3000

Chief Creative Officer: Jack Bishop
Editorial Director, Books: Elizabeth Carduff
Executive Editor: Julia Collin Davison
Executive Editor: Adam Kowit
Assistant Editor: Samantha Ronan
Design Director: Carole Goodman
Deputy Art Directors: Allison Boales and
Jen Kanavos Hoffman
Production Designer: Reinaldo Cruz
Graphic Designer: Katie Barranger
Photography Director: Julie Bozzo Cote
Photography Producer: Mary Ball
Senior Staff Photographer: Daniel J. van Ackere
Staff Photographer: Steve Klise
Feature Photography: Keller + Keller and Carl Tremblay
Food Styling: Catrine Kelty, Marie Piraino, Elle Simone Scott,
and Sally Staub
Photoshoot Kitchen Team:
   Senior Editor: Chris O'Connor
   Lead Cook: Daniel Cellucci
   Assistant Test Cooks: Mady Nichas and Jessica Rudolph
Production Director: Guy Rochford
Senior Production Manager: Jessica Lindheimer Quirk
Production Manager: Christine Walsh
Imaging Manager: Lauren Robbins
Production and Imaging Specialists: Heather Dube,
Sean MacDonald, Dennis Noble, and Jessica Voas
Copyeditor: Cheryl Redmond
Proofreader: Pat Jalbert-Levine
Indexer: Elizabeth Parson

Pictured on front cover: Herbed Roast Turkey (page 36), Make-
Ahead Turkey Gravy (page 47), Cranberry Chutney with Apples
and Crystallized Ginger (page 113), Whipped Potatoes (page 84)
Pictured on back cover: Glazed Spiral-Sliced Ham (page 51),
Baked Macaroni and Cheese (page 90), Chocolate Pots de
Crème (page 142), Green Salad with Orange Marmalade
Dressing and Toasted Almonds (page 26)

contents

welcome to america's test kitchen

THIS BOOK HAS BEEN TESTED, WRITTEN, AND EDITED BY THE FOLKS at America's Test Kitchen. Located in Boston's Seaport District in the historic Innovation and Design Building, it features 15,000 square feet of kitchen space including photography and video studios. It is the home of *Cook's Illustrated* magazine and *Cook's Country* magazine and is the Monday-through-Friday destination for more than 60 test cooks, editors, and cookware specialists. Our mission is to test recipes over and over again until we understand how and why they work and until we arrive at the "best" version.

We start the process of testing a recipe with a complete lack of preconceptions, which means that we accept no claim, no technique, and no recipe at face value. We simply assemble as many variations as possible, test a half-dozen of the most promising, and taste the results blind. We then construct our own recipe and continue to test it, varying ingredients, techniques, and cooking times until we reach a consensus. As we like to say in the test kitchen, "We make the mistakes so you don't have to." The result, we hope, is the best version of a particular recipe, but we realize that only you can be the final judge of our success (or failure). We use the same rigorous approach when we test equipment and taste ingredients.

All of this would not be possible without a belief that good cooking, much like good music, is based on a foundation of objective technique. Some people like spicy foods and others don't, but there is a right way to sauté, there is a best way to cook a pot roast, and there are measurable scientific principles involved in producing perfectly beaten, stable egg whites. Our ultimate goal is to investigate the fundamental principles of cooking to give you the techniques, tools, and ingredients you need to become a better cook. It is as simple as that.

To see what goes on behind the scenes at America's Test Kitchen, check out our social media channels for kitchen snapshots, exclusive content, video tips, and much more. You can watch us work (in our actual test kitchen) by tuning in to *America's Test Kitchen* or *Cook's Country from America's Test Kitchen* on public television or on our websites. Listen to test kitchen experts on public radio (SplendidTable.org) to hear insights that illuminate the truth about real home cooking. Want to hone your cooking skills or finally learn how to bake—with an America's Test Kitchen test cook? Enroll in one of our online cooking classes. If the big questions about the hows and whys of food science are your passion, join our Cook's Science experts for a deep dive. However you choose to visit us, we welcome you into our kitchen, where you can stand by our side as we test our way to the best recipes in America.

facebook.com/
AmericasTestKitchen

twitter.com/TestKitchen

youtube.com/
AmericasTestKitchen

instagram.com/TestKitchen

pinterest.com/TestKitchen

google.com/
+AmericasTestKitchen

AmericasTestKitchen.com
CooksIllustrated.com
CooksCountry.com
CooksScience.com
OnlineCookingSchool.com

introduction

CELEBRATIONS—BIG AND SMALL, FORMAL AND LAID BACK, TRADI-tional and offbeat—all center around one thing: the food. For many, the rich aroma of a hearty stuffing or the practice of readying a holiday turkey conjures instant memories even as new ones take root, weaving these beloved meals into cherished traditions. But before a meal can become tied to nostalgic memories, it needs to impress. During the holidays, the stakes can be high and the pressure intense. Few home cooks tackle a mammoth roast or a spectacular dessert with any regularity, so turning out these project dishes (as well as their necessary accompaniments) can prove intimidating. Enter this collection of recipes, a lifeline making the perfect celebratory feast not only possible, but a promise.

While most home cooks roast a turkey once a year at most, here in the test kitchen, preparing this big bird is an art we have mastered and remastered over decades of rigorous recipe testing. The try-and-try-again treatment we apply to all of our recipes is even more stringent when it comes to holiday-caliber dishes, because when you're working with a pricey cut of meat or you're tasked with peeling a mountain of potatoes, you want your labor to be worth it. The 75 recipes compiled here are guaranteed to surpass expectations. They range from upgraded standbys (like our light, fluffy, and satisfyingly buttery Whipped Potatoes, page 84, or our stream-lined skillet-only Quick Green Bean "Casserole," page 107) to unexpected new favorites (like our ultramodern and entirely fuss-free Quick Tarte Tatin with Pears, page 151, finished off with a silky caramel sauce and tangy whipped cream). We show you how to pack your sky-high Deep-Dish Apple Pie (page 153) with sweet-tart apples (not gaps), and we prove that fresh rolls can be baked ahead of time with our light-as-air Fluffy Dinner Rolls (page 131). And while we have an impressive range of turkey recipes to suit all needs, the bird is just the beginning. The Centerpieces chapter show-cases the depth of *Cook's Illustrated*'s repertoire, offering everything from our luscious Onion-Braised Beef Brisket (page 61) to the heavily spiced, supertender Italian-inspired Porchetta (page 58). And we haven't forgotten our vegetarian guests: With entrées like Fennel, Olive, and Goat Cheese Tarts (page 78) and a wide array of meatless starters and sides to choose from, you will have little trouble pleasing everyone at the table.

We simplify your planning by dividing the recipes across four chapters— Starters, Centerpieces, Shareable Sides, and Sweet Endings—so whether you're building a meal around a singular roast or you have been asked to fill in the gaps in a family potluck, you'll know exactly where to look. No great feast ever materialized in a single afternoon, so many of these recipes fea-ture make-ahead information, allowing you to prep everything from soup to soufflés well before the doorbell rings, and we've outlined a rough timeline to make planning even easier.

So before you put on your hosting hat, be our guest: Allow *Cook's Illustrated* to show you how to make entertaining an enjoyable, exhilarating experience this year. Your friends and family will thank you later.

here come the holidays

the holiday playbook

Whether it's your first rodeo or you're a seasoned host, entertaining is a lot of work. Assembling the guest list and tidying the house come with their own pressures, but for most people, building a menu, preparing large amounts of food, and determining how to get everything onto the table in time are what keep home cooks up at night. Fear not: This timeline breaks down when you can tackle each task for a perfectly executed celebration.

three weeks ahead

pick your protein Finalize your guest list, determine the tone you want your celebration to take, and then pick out a fitting centerpiece protein. Turkeys and specialty roasts are an investment and require preordering, so take care of this first.

refresh your spice rack Toss out old jars of spices and dried herbs and stock up on replacements. Check that you have enough salt and pepper, both for cooking and for filling shakers.

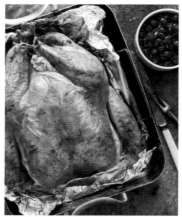

track down your tools Inventory your essential kitchen equipment, serving implements, dinnerware, glassware, and linens to make sure you are well stocked.

test kitchen–inspired entertaining

hosting all the aunts, uncles, and cousins? The massive bird used in our Roast Turkey for a Crowd (page 38) will satisfy up to 24 people and is best ordered well ahead of time. Use your big-format feast as an opportunity to try out a wide range of savory sides.

hoping for a christmas feast with a more dickensian feel? Cozy up to Britain's beloved Boneless Rib Roast with Yorkshire Pudding (page 64), a traditional meal that pairs custardy pudding with enough juicy roast beef to satisfy up to 10 people.

throwing a southern-inspired soirée? Order yourself a spiral-sliced bone-in half ham, check out our sweet and salty Glazed Spiral-Sliced Ham (page 51), and pair it with ham's favorite side: Baked Macaroni and Cheese (page 90).

gathering a small group of friends for new year's? Pan-Seared Duck Breasts with Dried Cherry Sauce (page 70) is an elegant, small-scale main, and our Asparagus with Lemon-Shallot Vinaigrette (page 98) makes for a stylish accompaniment.

two weeks ahead

fill your freezer Prepare items that can afford a long spell in the freezer, like pie, tart, and cookie doughs, or our make-ahead Chocolate Soufflés (page 144). If you don't want to use giblets in your gravy, freeze it; the base for our Make-Ahead Turkey Gravy (page 47) can be frozen a month ahead.

load up your pantry Stock up on canned pumpkin (our favorite is Libby's 100% Pure Pumpkin), chicken broth (we recommend Swanson Chicken Stock), sugar, flour, oil, vinegar, and frozen vegetables.

with days to go

give your turkey time Don't underestimate how long it takes a turkey to defrost! Give your frozen turkey one day of thawing for every 4 pounds, timing it so your bird finishes defrosting a day before roasting (leaving you time to air-dry the turkey in the refrigerator for crisp skin).

hit the produce and dairy aisles A week out, stock up on vegetables that store well, like onions, garlic, potatoes, sweet potatoes, root vegetables, and squash. Save more delicate items like fresh herbs until you're within just a few days of cooking. Make sure you have enough milk and cream for all of your recipes, and pick up plenty of butter, unsalted for cooking and salted if you plan on serving dinner rolls.

ready your salad greens Crisp, sturdy heads like radicchio or romaine can be cored, wrapped in moist paper towels, and stored in a zipper-lock bag left slightly open for up to a week. Inspect prewashed leafy greens like mesclun and arugula before purchasing, looking for moisture or blackened leaves, and keep them in their original packaging.

think starters and sides Once you're within two to three days, begin preparing warm dips, cranberry sauce, and vinaigrettes for salads, storing them covered in the refrigerator.

the day before

assemble your baked goods Ready those remaining items that can be prepared early and baked or warmed up just before serving, like casseroles, stuffings, and pies.

brine and salt Brining and air-drying turkey or salting roasts like our Slow-Roasted Fresh Ham (page 52) or Porchetta (page 58) is best done with 24 hours to go.

get peeling Peel potatoes and then submerge them in water in the refrigerator—this will make preparing Garlic Mashed Potatoes (page 86) or Whipped Potatoes (page 84) more manageable the next day.

review your game plan, and rest up Before you turn in for the night, review your recipes and calculate how long your centerpiece will occupy the oven and leave yourself enough time to heat up your prepared sides. Set your alarm accordingly and get some sleep.

the big day

get fired up and chill out Preheat the oven and pop your cold beverages in the refrigerator. Make sure you have plenty of ice for drinks.

roast and rest Roast your protein, keeping in mind that many roasts require some resting time in addition to cooking time.

get fresh While your roast is in the oven and resting, prepare fresh vegetable sides and finish off those items you partially prepped ahead of time. Salads can be assembled, but delay dressing them until serving.

dot your i's, cross your t's Make sure the finishing touches are in place by setting the table, dusting off your serving platters, polishing glasses, and emptying your trash and recycling bins.

---

an effortless last-minute napkin fold

1. Fold square napkin in half, and then in half again, creating long rectangle.

2. With seams facing up, fold one short end two-thirds of the way in. Fold opposite end in so two short ends meet.

3. Fold napkin where seams of two short ends meet and press to flatten.

equip your kitchen

We refuse to break the bank on pieces we only use a few times a year. These essential tools are useful year-round and worth the expense:

roasting pan
Handsome and heavy-duty, this roomy pan is essential to preparing hefty turkeys and roasts. Our favorite: **Calphalon Contemporary Stainless Roasting Pan with Rack** ($99.99)

instant-read thermometer
The holidays are no time for guesswork, so keep an accurate thermometer on hand. Our favorites: **ThermoWorks Thermapen Mk4** ($99) and **Thermoworks ThermoPop** ($29).

oven thermometer
Arming your oven with a thermometer is the best (and only) way to know when it's properly preheated. Our favorite: **CDN Pro Accurate Oven Thermometer** ($8.70).

carving fork
This tool holds roasts in place while carving and makes for neater serving. Our favorite: **Mercer Culinary Genesis 6" High-Carbon Carving Fork** ($22.20).

slicing knife
The long, thin blade of this knife makes slicing a large roast safe and easy. Our favorite: **Victorinox 12" Fibrox Pro Granton Edge Slicing/ Carving Knife** ($54.65).

carving board
Designed with trenches to contain escaping drippings and a well to hold a roast in place, this board is a holiday essential. Our favorite: **J.K. Adams Maple Reversible Carving Board** ($69.95).

tart pan
Models with removable bottoms work best, and a dark, nonstick coating makes for deep browning and a clean release. Our favorite: **Matfer Steel Non-Stick Fluted Tart Mold** ($27).

springform pan
Pick a pan with a wide, flat base and tight latched collar. Gold-toned pans produce evenly baked crusts. Our favorite: **Williams-Sonoma Goldtouch Springform Pan, 9"** ($49.95).

pie server
Don't mangle your perfect pie (or tart or cake); use a server sharp enough to cut through crust and agile enough to neatly transport slices. Our favorite: **OXO Steel Pie Server** ($9.99).

holiday hosting 911

We are no strangers to kitchen mishaps, but over the years we've also come up with a host of quick and easy solutions to common crises plus a few clever tricks for an impressive presentation.

pack it up, pack it in

Large gatherings often call for food to hit the road. Here are our transport tips, whether you're hosting or attending.

rolling in with a casserole

The best way to safely tote a piping hot casserole along to its final destination is in an insulated food carrier. We rely on the **Rachael Ray Expandable Lasagna Lugger** ($26.95) when we are bringing dishes like our Mushroom Lasagna (page 81) or Homemade Cornbread Dressing (page 116) along to the party. It's capable of keeping food nice and hot for up to 3 hours.

send them packing

Guests love taking leftovers home, but it's painful to part with pricey containers that you know you'll never see again. Send folks home happy is by picking up a few packages of inexpensive plastic containers and letting guests fill them up before hitting the road. We like to set out a few stacks of **Gladware Deep Dish** ($5.97) containers and **Ziploc Brand Freezer Bags with Easy Open Tabs** ($5.37 for 28 bags) at the end of the meal.

expand your counter space

Envious of kitchens with miles of counter space and pullout cutting boards? Hack your own by placing a cutting board or cookie sheet over an opened drawer. Use it as a surface for prepping lightweight ingredients or for supporting bowls. No matter the size of the kitchen, a little extra space for resting bowls, platters, or cooling racks never hurts. And when it comes time to cool cookies, extend counter space by setting the cooling racks directly over the sink, which has the added benefit of making it easy to clean up the crumbs that fall through the rack. (We don't recommend this tip for households with young children running about.)

tidy up a greasy spill

A greasy spill is both tedious to clean up and dangerous if not done well. Rather than trying to wipe up the mess with numerous rolls of paper towels, try this solution: Sprinkle a thick layer of flour over the grease spill, and let it absorb for a couple of minutes. The greasy flour can then be easily swept up and the floor cleaned quickly with window cleaner.

resurrect an undercooked roast

You've roasted, rested, and sliced up the meat, only to find it much too rare. Obviously, you need to return the meat to the oven to finish cooking, but the trick here is to prevent the meat from drying out and turning gray. Our solution is to place the slices of meat on a wire rack set in a rimmed baking sheet, top with pieces of lettuce, and finish the cooking under the broiler. The meat will gently steam under the lettuce, without drying out.

warm your dinner plates

Warmed plates or bowls are particularly nice when serving soups, stews, or pasta dishes. Stack them on a clean cookie sheet and warm them in a low oven. If, however, your oven is in use, consider using the drying cycle on the dishwasher to warm them up.

mend cracked cheesecake

Even when every precaution is taken, the occasional cheesecake will develop unsightly cracks. Here's a simple method for repairing them.

1. Remove the sidewall from the springform pan while the cheesecake is warm. Wrap a cloth ribbon snugly around the cake, preferably one that covers the sides completely (about 3 inches wide for most pans).

2. Secure the ribbon with a binder clip, and leave in place until the cake has cooled completely.

aerate wine in a flash

If you don't have enough time to let a young bottle of red breathe, fear not. You can quickly aerate your wine (giving it instant bright, complex flavor) by pouring between two pitchers 15 times.

unwhip overwhipped cream

If you accidentally go too far and overwhip the cream, try this trick to ensure all is not lost.

1. Add unwhipped cream to the overwhipped mixture 1 tablespoon at a time.

2. Gently fold in, adding more unwhipped cream until the desired consistency is reached.

stabilize weepy whipped cream

Cream begins to break down soon after whipping. To prepare whipped cream in advance, try adding marshmallow crème to keep it stable. Whip in 6 tablespoons of crème for every cup of heavy cream, along with ½ teaspoon of rum extract or vanilla extract. Cover and refrigerate. The crème keeps the cream from deflating for up to a day and also adds a pleasantly sweet marshmallow flavor.

save some for yourself

Half the pleasure of preparing an exceptional feast for friends and family is enjoying the leftovers the next day. Store the remains **Kinetic Go Green GlassLock** ($7.99) or **Snapware Airtight** ($7.99) containers, both perfect for preserving food in the refrigerator and safe for reheating in the microwave.

To reheat your turkey and gravy, place leftover slices in a steamer basket set in a pot of simmering water, then cover the pot with a lid and check it every few minutes. The turkey heats up quickly and stays juicy. Alternatively, you can wrap leftover portions in aluminum foil, stacking any sliced pieces, and place them on a wire rack set in a rimmed baking sheet. Transfer to a 275-degree oven and heat until the meat registers 130 degrees. Timing will vary based on the shape and size of the leftover turkey pieces.

If you have large skin-on pieces, place them skin side down in a lightly oiled skillet over medium-high heat, heating until the skin recrisps.

Refrigerated or frozen gravy can be resuscitated by bringing it to a full boil and whisking vigorously until it returns to its thick, emulsified consistency.

cheers!

Festive libations are a must at holiday gatherings. In addition to a selection of wines, liquors, and soft drinks, we suggest having one (or more!) of our spirited beverages on offer at your next soirée.

mulled wine

serves 8

Merlot, Pinot Noir, or Côtes du Rhône will work here. The wine's flavor will deteriorate if simmered more than 1 hour. Mulled wine will remain fairly hot off the heat, covered, for about 30 minutes.

3 cinnamon sticks

10 whole cloves

10 whole peppercorns

1 teaspoon allspice berries

2 (750 ml) bottles red wine

4 (2-inch) strips orange zest

½ cup plus 2 tablespoons sugar

2–4 tablespoons brandy

1. Toast cinnamon sticks, cloves, peppercorns, and allspice in medium saucepan over medium-high heat until fragrant, about 2 minutes. Add wine, orange zest, and ½ cup sugar; cover partially and bring to simmer, stirring occasionally to dissolve sugar. Reduce heat to low and simmer 1 hour until wine is infused; do not boil.

2. Line fine-mesh strainer with triple layer of cheesecloth and set over large bowl. Pour wine through prepared strainer and discard solids. Return wine to saucepan. Stir 2 tablespoons brandy into wine; taste and add up to 2 tablespoons more sugar and 2 tablespoons more brandy, if desired. Serve immediately.

fireside mulled cider
serves 16 to 18

1 gallon apple cider

2 oranges, sliced ½ inch thick

1 lemon, sliced ½ inch thick

1 (2-inch) piece ginger, sliced ¼ inch thick

2 teaspoons allspice berries

6 whole cloves

1 teaspoon black peppercorns

1 cinnamon stick

1. Bring all ingredients to boil in Dutch oven over medium-high heat. Reduce heat to low and steep for 30 minutes.

2. Line fine-mesh strainer with triple layer of cheesecloth and set over large bowl. Pour mulled cider through prepared strainer and discard solids. Return cider to pot and keep warm over low heat. Serve.

irish coffee
serves 4
For sweet, creamy coffee, add 1 tablespoon of Bailey's Irish Cream to each mug.

½ cup Irish whiskey

4 cups fresh brewed coffee, hot

Sugar (optional)

1 recipe Whipped Cream (page 147)

Pour 2 tablespoons whiskey into each of 4 large mugs. Fill mugs with coffee. Season with sugar, if desired, and dollop with whipped cream before serving.

eggnog
serves 6 to 8

1½ cups heavy cream

6 large egg yolks

6 tablespoons sugar

3 cups whole milk

¼ teaspoon salt

½ cup dark rum

¼ teaspoon ground nutmeg, plus extra for serving

1. Whisk ¾ cup cream, egg yolks, and sugar in medium bowl until thoroughly combined and pale yellow, about 30 seconds; set aside. Bring milk and salt to simmer in medium saucepan over medium-high heat, stirring occasionally.

2. When milk mixture comes to simmer, remove from heat and, whisking constantly, slowly pour into yolk mixture to temper. Return milk-yolk mixture to saucepan. Place over medium-low heat and cook, whisking constantly, until mixture reaches 160 degrees, 1 to 2 minutes.

3. Immediately pour eggnog into clean bowl. Stir in rum and nutmeg. Fill slightly larger bowl with ice and set eggnog bowl in ice bowl. Refrigerate until eggnog registers 40 degrees, 1 to 2 hours, stirring occasionally.

4. Just before serving, using stand mixer fitted with whisk attachment, whip remaining ¾ cup cream on medium-low speed until foamy, about 1 minute. Increase speed to high and whip until soft peaks form, 1 to 3 minutes. Whisk whipped cream into chilled eggnog. Serve, garnished with extra nutmeg.

champagne punch
serves 20 to 25
To ensure a properly chilled punch, keep all the ingredients in the refrigerator before beginning the recipe. Sauvignon Blanc works well here. We like to scatter a few fresh mint leaves in the punch bowl just before serving for added color and flavor.

2 (750-ml) bottles extra-dry Champagne or sparkling wine, cold

1 (750-ml) bottle fruity white wine, cold

1½ quarts unsweetened pineapple juice, cold

1 quart lemonade, cold

Stir Champagne, white wine, juice, and lemonade together in large punch bowl until well combined. Serve immediately over ice, if desired.

variations
pink champagne punch
Substitute 2 bottles rosé Champagne or sparkling wine for Champagne, 1 bottle white Zinfandel for white wine, pink grapefruit juice for pineapple juice, and pink lemonade for lemonade.

sparkling punch (nonalcoholic)
Substitute 3 (750-ml) bottles sparkling apple cider or 1 (2-liter) bottle lemon-lime soda for alcohol.

starters

roasted artichoke dip

why this recipe works Putting out an easy, appealing dip as soon as guests arrive is the best way to keep hungry diners out of the kitchen as you finish preparing the meal. This retro favorite remains an irresistible crowd-pleaser, loaded with distinct artichoke flavor under a golden, crispy crust. For a simple, freshened-up take that could easily be made ahead of time, we replaced tinny canned artichokes with the cleaner taste of frozen and roasted them to intensify their flavor. A combination of mayonnaise and cream cheese for our base gave the dip a creamy, rich texture, and sprinkling on a Parmesan–bread crumb topping made for a crunchy, savory finishing touch. Do not thaw the frozen artichoke hearts. This dip is best served warm. Serve with crackers or a thinly sliced baguette.

serves 8 to 10
total time: 1 hour 15 minutes

topping
2 slices hearty white sandwich bread, torn into quarters

2 tablespoons grated Parmesan cheese

1 tablespoon unsalted butter, melted

dip
18 ounces frozen artichokes

2 tablespoons olive oil

Salt and pepper

1 onion, chopped fine

2 garlic cloves, minced

1 cup mayonnaise

4 ounces cream cheese, softened

1 ounce Parmesan cheese, grated (½ cup)

2 tablespoons lemon juice

1 tablespoon minced fresh thyme

Pinch cayenne pepper

1. for the topping Pulse bread in food processor until coarsely ground, about 12 pulses. Toss bread crumbs with Parmesan and melted butter; set aside.

2. for the dip Adjust oven rack to middle position and heat oven to 450 degrees. Line rimmed baking sheet with aluminum foil. Toss artichokes with 1 tablespoon oil, ½ teaspoon salt, and ¼ teaspoon pepper on prepared sheet. Roast artichokes, stirring occasionally, until browned at edges, about 25 minutes. When cool enough to handle, chop artichokes coarse. Reduce oven temperature to 400 degrees.

3. Meanwhile, heat remaining 1 tablespoon oil in 10-inch skillet over medium-high heat until just shimmering. Add onion and cook until softened, 5 to 7 minutes. Stir in garlic and cook until fragrant, about 30 seconds. Transfer onion mixture to large bowl.

4. Stir mayonnaise, cream cheese, Parmesan, lemon juice, thyme, and cayenne into onion mixture until uniform, smearing any lumps of cream cheese against side of bowl with rubber spatula. Gently fold in artichokes and season with salt and pepper to taste. Transfer mixture to 1-quart baking dish and smooth top. Sprinkle topping evenly over dip.

5. Bake dip until hot throughout and topping is golden brown, 20 to 25 minutes. Let dip cool for 5 minutes before serving.

to make ahead
Unbaked dip can be covered tightly with plastic wrap and refrigerated for up to 3 days.

herbed spinach dip

why this recipe works Spinach dip can feel like the healthy choice among appetizers, but that doesn't mean it has to be bland. For a spinach dip that pleased everyone at the table, we ramped up the flavor with fresh, fragrant herbs, sweet red bell pepper, scallions, garlic, and some hot sauce for a little extra kick. To combine these disparate ingredients evenly and with ease, we used the food processor to help distribute the spinach evenly throughout the dip. This method also made it easy to add other flavors to the dip for a few creative variations. The garlic must be minced or pressed before going into the food processor or the dip will contain large chunks of garlic. Serve with crudités.

serves 9
total time: 15 minutes
(plus 1 hour for chilling)

10 ounces frozen chopped spinach, thawed and squeezed dry

½ red bell pepper, chopped fine

½ cup sour cream

½ cup mayonnaise

½ cup fresh parsley leaves

3 scallions, sliced thin

1 tablespoon chopped fresh dill or 1 teaspoon dried

1 garlic clove, minced

¼ teaspoon hot sauce

Salt and pepper

Process all ingredients with ½ teaspoon salt and ¼ teaspoon pepper in food processor until well combined, about 1 minute. Transfer to serving bowl, cover, and refrigerate until flavors have blended, at least 1 hour. Season with salt and pepper to taste before serving.

variations

spinach dip with blue cheese and bacon

Omit bell pepper, dill, hot sauce, and salt. Add ⅓ cup crumbled blue cheese to food processor with spinach. Sprinkle with 2 slices cooked, crumbled bacon before serving.

spinach dip with feta, lemon, and oregano

Omit bell pepper, dill, and salt. Add ½ cup crumbled feta cheese, 2 tablespoons fresh oregano leaves, 1 teaspoon grated lemon zest, and 1 tablespoon lemon juice to food processor with spinach. Season with salt to taste before serving.

cilantro–lime spinach dip

Omit bell pepper, dill, and hot sauce. Add ¼ cup fresh cilantro leaves, 1 tablespoon chopped canned chipotle chile in adobo sauce, ½ teaspoon grated lime zest, 1 tablespoon lime juice, ½ teaspoon light brown sugar, and ⅛ teaspoon ground cumin to food processor with spinach.

to make ahead
Dip can be refrigerated for up to 24 hours.

chicken liver pâté

why this recipe works This smooth, buttery pâté is the perfect way to start off an elegant holiday meal. To keep this indulgent spread as simple as possible, we began by sautéing shallots in butter with fresh thyme and vermouth for an aromatic base. We seared the livers to build their flavor and then gently poached them to ensure a moist pâté. A bit of brandy unified the pâté's flavors. Pressing plastic wrap against the surface of the pâté before refrigerating it minimized any discoloration from oxidation. Buy the freshest livers possible and make sure to trim them of fat and connective tissues. Serve with toast points, crackers, or a sliced baguette, and cornichons.

serves 6 to 8
total time: 30 minutes
(plus 6 hours for chilling)

8 tablespoons unsalted butter

3 large shallots, sliced thin

1 tablespoon minced fresh thyme

Salt and pepper

1 pound chicken livers, rinsed, patted dry, and trimmed of fat and connective tissue

¾ cup dry vermouth

2 teaspoons brandy

1. Melt butter in 12-inch skillet over medium-high heat. Add shallots, thyme, and ¼ teaspoon salt and cook until shallots are lightly browned, 3 to 5 minutes. Add chicken livers and cook, stirring constantly, about 1 minute. Add vermouth and simmer until livers have rosy interior, 4 to 6 minutes.

2. Using slotted spoon, transfer livers to food processor. Continue to simmer vermouth mixture until slightly syrupy, 2 minutes.

3. Add vermouth mixture and brandy to processor. Process mixture until very smooth, about 2 minutes, scraping down bowl as needed. Season with salt and pepper to taste. Transfer to small serving bowl, smooth top, press plastic wrap flush to surface of pâté, and refrigerate until firm, at least 6 hours.

4. Before serving, bring to room temperature to soften, and scrape off any discolored pâté on top.

to make ahead
Pâté can be refrigerated for up to 3 days.

brie en croûte

why this recipe works The combination of warm, creamy Brie encased in a flaky puff pastry crust with sweet jam sets a rich, refined tone for any cold-weather feast. We love this cheese plate centerpiece because, while it's certainly impressive, it could hardly be easier to prepare. Working with a firm wheel of Brie promised gooey cheese that still held its shape under a fuss-free puff pastry shell. A quick stint in the freezer before baking ensured just the right consistency at serving time: soft and melted but not oily or runny. To thaw frozen puff pastry, allow it to sit either in the refrigerator for 24 hours or on the counter for 30 to 60 minutes. It is best to use a firm, fairly unripe Brie for this recipe. Serve with crackers.

serves 8
total time: 1 hour
(plus 30 minutes for cooling)

1 (9½ by 9-inch) sheet frozen puff pastry, thawed

1 large egg, lightly beaten

1 (8-ounce) wheel firm Brie cheese

¼ cup fig, apricot, or cranberry jam

1. Roll puff pastry into 12-inch square on lightly floured counter. Using 9-inch round plate (or pie plate) as guide, trim pastry into 9-inch circle with paring knife. Brush edges lightly with beaten egg. Place Brie in center of pastry circle and wrap in pastry, lifting pastry up over cheese, pleating it at even intervals, and leaving opening in center where Brie is exposed. Press pleated edge of pastry up to form rim. Brush exterior of pastry with beaten egg.

2. Adjust oven rack to middle position and heat oven to 425 degrees. Line rimmed baking sheet with parchment paper. Transfer Brie to prepared baking sheet and freeze for 20 minutes. Bake cheese until exterior is deep golden brown, 20 to 25 minutes.

3. Transfer cheese to wire rack. Spoon jam into exposed center of Brie and let cool for about 30 minutes before serving.

to make ahead
Unbaked Brie can be wrapped tightly in plastic wrap and refrigerated for up to 24 hours.

wrapping brie in puff pastry

1. Lift pastry up over Brie, pleating at even intervals and leaving opening in center where Brie is exposed.

2. Press pleated edge of pastry up to form small rim.

creamy cauliflower soup

why this recipe works Thanks to cauliflower's natural ability to turn into a lush puree without the addition of cream, this simple soup shines with the multifaceted flavors of cauliflower, offering an elegant start to any meal without spoiling your appetite. We kept the cauliflower front and center by cooking it in water and skipping the spice rack entirely, bolstering the soup with sautéed onion and leek. We simmered in two stages to unlock the grassy flavor of just-cooked cauliflower as well as the sweeter, nuttier taste of longer-cooked cauliflower. For a festive, flavorful garnish, we browned butter and more florets to top off each serving. White wine vinegar may be substituted for the sherry vinegar. Be sure to thoroughly trim the cauliflower's core of green leaves and leaf stems, which can be fibrous and contribute to a grainy texture in the soup.

serves 3 to 12
total time: 1 hour 15 minutes

2 heads cauliflower
(2 pounds each)

16 tablespoons (2 sticks) unsalted butter, cut into 16 pieces

2 leeks, white and light green parts only, halved lengthwise, sliced thin, and washed thoroughly

1 onion, halved and sliced thin

Salt and pepper

9 cups water, plus extra as needed

1½ teaspoons sherry vinegar

⅓ cup minced fresh chives

1. Pull off outer leaves of cauliflower and trim stems. Using paring knife, cut around core to remove; slice core thin and reserve. Cut heaping 3 cups of ½-inch florets from heads of cauliflower; set aside. Cut remaining cauliflower crosswise into ½-inch-thick slices.

2. Melt 6 tablespoons butter in Dutch oven over medium-low heat. Add leeks, onion, and 1½ teaspoons salt; cook, stirring frequently, until leeks and onion are softened but not browned, about 7 minutes.

3. Increase heat to medium-high; add water, sliced cores, and half of sliced cauliflower; and bring to simmer. Reduce heat to medium-low and simmer gently for 15 minutes. Add remaining sliced cauliflower, return to simmer, and continue to cook until cauliflower is tender and crumbles easily, 15 to 20 minutes longer.

4. Working in batches, process soup in blender until smooth, about 45 seconds. Rinse out pan. Return pureed soup to pan and return to simmer over medium heat, adjusting consistency with extra hot water as needed (soup should have thick, velvety texture but should be thin enough to settle with flat surface after being stirred) and seasoning with salt to taste.

5. While soup simmers, melt remaining 10 tablespoons butter in 12-inch skillet over medium heat. Add reserved florets and cook, stirring frequently, until florets are golden brown and butter is browned and imparts nutty aroma, 10 to 12 minutes. Remove skillet from heat and use slotted spoon to transfer florets to small bowl. Toss florets with vinegar and season with salt to taste. Pour browned butter in skillet into small bowl and reserve for garnishing.

6. Serve, garnishing individual bowls with browned florets, drizzle of browned butter, and chives and seasoning with pepper to taste.

to make ahead
Soup, prepared through step 4, can be refrigerated for up to 3 days. To serve, bring soup to gentle simmer, covered, stirring often. Adjust consistency with hot water as needed and continue with step 5.

sweet potato soup

why this recipe works The secret to our creamy sweet potato soup's deep, earthy-sweet flavor? Keeping the skins in play. Before simmering and pureeing the peeled potatoes, we coaxed out more natural sweetness by soaking them in hot water, allowing their starches to turn into pure sugar. Pureeing some of the skins along with the softened potatoes added depth to the otherwise sweet soup, a contrast we reinforced with some brown sugar and a touch of cider vinegar. Along with the chives, serve the soup with one of our suggested garnishes below.

serves 8
total time: 1 hour

4 tablespoons unsalted butter

1 shallot, sliced thin

4 sprigs fresh thyme

4¼ cups water

2 pounds sweet potatoes, peeled, halved lengthwise, and sliced ¼ inch thick, one-quarter of peels reserved

1 tablespoon packed brown sugar

½ teaspoon cider vinegar

Salt and pepper

Minced fresh chives

1. Melt butter in large saucepan over medium-low heat. Add shallot and thyme sprigs and cook until shallot is softened but not browned, about 5 minutes. Add water, increase heat to high, and bring to simmer. Remove pot from heat, add sweet potatoes and reserved peels, and let stand uncovered for 20 minutes.

2. Add sugar, vinegar, 1½ teaspoons salt, and ¼ teaspoon pepper. Bring to simmer over high heat. Reduce heat to medium-low, cover, and cook until potatoes are very soft, about 10 minutes.

3. Discard thyme sprigs. Working in batches, process soup in blender until smooth, 45 to 60 seconds. Return soup to clean pot.

4. Bring to simmer over medium heat, adjusting consistency if desired. Season with salt and pepper to taste. Serve, topping each portion with sprinkle of chives.

candied bacon bits
makes about ¼ cup
Break up any large chunks before serving.

4 slices bacon, cut into ½-inch pieces

2 teaspoons packed dark brown sugar

½ teaspoon cider vinegar

Cook bacon in 10-inch nonstick skillet over medium heat until crisp and well rendered, 6 to 8 minutes. Using slotted spoon, remove bacon from skillet and discard fat. Return bacon to skillet and add brown sugar and vinegar. Cook over low heat, stirring constantly, until bacon is evenly coated. Transfer to plate in single layer. Let bacon cool completely.

buttery rye croutons
makes 1½ cups
These croutons are made in a skillet; they can be made ahead and stored for one week.

3 tablespoons unsalted butter

1 tablespoon olive oil

2 slices light rye bread, cut into ½-inch cubes (1½ cups)

Salt

Heat butter and oil in 10-inch skillet over medium heat until butter melts. Add bread cubes and cook, stirring frequently, until golden brown, about 10 minutes. Transfer croutons to paper towel–lined plate and season with salt to taste.

maple sour cream
makes ⅓ cup

⅓ cup sour cream

1 tablespoon maple syrup

Combine ingredients in bowl.

to make ahead
Soup, prepared through step 3, can be refrigerated for up to 3 days. To serve, bring soup to gentle simmer, covered, stirring often. Adjust consistency with hot water as needed and continue with step 4.

rich and velvety shrimp bisque

why this recipe works This soup is pure elegance, putting shrimp's natural sweetness on display. For a bisque that set the tone for a holiday meal, we coarsely ground a full 2 pounds of shell-on shrimp in a food processor to extract every drop of flavor, then cooked them with mirepoix, melted butter, and herbs to build a fragrant base. Dry white wine plus chopped tomatoes and some of their juice brightened the base, which we simmered at length to concentrate flavors before straining. Just before serving, we poached more shrimp right in the bisque until tender and juicy, and added a dollop of whipped cream to put this starter over the top.

serves 12
total time: 2 hours

2 carrots, peeled and chopped coarse

2 celery ribs, chopped coarse

1 onion, chopped coarse

3 garlic cloves, peeled

3 pounds extra-large shell-on shrimp (21 to 25 per pound), 2 pounds left shell-on, 1 pound peeled and deveined

4 tablespoons unsalted butter

3 sprigs fresh thyme

2 bay leaves

Salt and pepper

½ teaspoon sugar

1¼ cups all-purpose flour

5 (8-ounce) bottles clam juice

3 cups dry white wine

1¾ cups chicken broth

1¾ cups vegetable broth

1 (28-ounce) can diced tomatoes, drained, ¼ cup juice reserved

1½ cups heavy cream

¼ cup dry sherry or Madeira

2 tablespoons lemon juice

Pinch cayenne pepper

¼ tablespoon minced fresh chives

1. Pulse carrots, celery, onion, and garlic in food processor until finely chopped, about 5 pulses; transfer to bowl and set aside. Process 1 pound shell-on shrimp (with shells) in food processor until finely chopped, 10 to 15 seconds; transfer to bowl with vegetables and repeat with remaining 1 pound shell-on shrimp.

2. Melt butter in Dutch oven over medium-high heat. Stir in chopped vegetables and shrimp, thyme sprigs, bay leaves, 1 teaspoon salt, and sugar. Cover and cook, stirring frequently, until shrimp are pink and have released their juices and vegetables are softened, about 10 minutes.

3. Stir in flour and cook, stirring constantly, until thoroughly combined and lightly browned, about 1 minute. Stir in clam juice, wine, broths, tomatoes, and ¼ cup reserved tomato juice. Cover and bring to boil. Uncover, reduce to simmer, and cook, stirring frequently, until broth is thickened, 50 minutes to 1 hour.

4. Strain broth through colander, pressing on solids with back of ladle to extract liquid (you should have just under 3 quarts). Strain broth again, to remove any fine bits, through fine-mesh strainer (or colander lined with a double layer of damp cheesecloth).

5. Transfer broth to Dutch oven and bring to simmer over medium heat, about 15 minutes. Meanwhile, whip ½ cup of cream to stiff peaks and season with salt and pepper to taste; set aside.

6. Stir remaining 1 cup cream, peeled and deveined shrimp, sherry, lemon juice, and cayenne into broth and simmer until shrimp are just pink, about 1 minute. Remove from heat and season with salt and pepper to taste When serving, dollop individual portions with whipped cream and sprinkle with chives.

to make ahead
Strained broth can be refrigerated for up to 2 days following step 4.

green salad with orange marmalade dressing and toasted almonds

why this recipe works A green salad offers just the right light touch to kick off a big meal, but simple doesn't have to mean boring. For a colorful, texturally interesting salad, we carefully selected a few distinctive ingredients. Pairing peppery arugula with tender mesclun greens made a good starting place. Mixing tangy-sweet orange marmalade and nutty-tasting sherry vinegar into a vinaigrette proved an easy way to give the greens an instant boost. Crunchy sliced radishes and toasted almonds offered an elegant finish to this appealing, straightforward salad. Toast the almonds in a skillet (without any oil) set over medium heat, shaking the pan occasionally to prevent scorching.

serves 12
total time: 15 minutes

dressing

3 tablespoons orange marmalade

3 tablespoons sherry or red wine vinegar

1 shallot, minced

1 teaspoon minced fresh thyme

Salt and pepper

6 tablespoons extra-virgin olive oil

salad

5 ounces (5 cups) baby arugula

5 ounces (5 cups) mesclun greens

8 radishes, trimmed and sliced thin

1 cup sliced almonds, toasted

1. for the dressing Whisk marmalade, vinegar, shallot, thyme, ½ teaspoon salt, and ¼ teaspoon pepper together in a medium bowl. Whisking constantly, drizzle in oil.

2. for the salad Toss salad greens and radishes together in large bowl, cover with damp paper towels, and refrigerate until needed. Just before serving, whisk dressing to re-emulsify, then drizzle over salad and toss gently to coat. Sprinkle with almonds and serve.

to make ahead

Vinaigrette can be refrigerated for up to 2 days. Let refrigerated vinaigrette sit at room temperature to allow oil to liquefy before dressing salad. Salad greens and radishes can be tossed in large serving bowl, covered with damp paper towels, and refrigerated up to 6 hours ahead of time.

brussels sprout salad with warm bacon vinaigrette

why this recipe works In order to turn Brussels sprout leaves into a tender, appealing wintertime salad, all we needed was a little heat and some impactful mix-ins. To bring refinement to the simple hand-sliced sprouts, we quickly pickled mellow sliced shallots in red wine vinegar and whole-grain mustard, warming the mixture in the microwave to infuse the shallots with flavor. To turn the pickling liquid into a complex vinaigrette, we crisped slices of bacon and whisked in the shallots and vinegar mixture, the bacon and its still-hot renderings offering instant smoky, salty flavor. We tossed the shredded sprouts in the warm vinaigrette, allowing the leaves to soften and wilt while taking on plenty of flavor. Shredded radicchio added some contrasting color and crunch, and serving the salad with shaved Parmesan and toasted almonds gave this deeply savory starter some extra distinction. A food processor's slicing blade can be used to slice the Brussels sprouts, but the salad will be less tender. Toast the almonds in a skillet (without any oil) set over medium heat, shaking the pan occasionally to prevent scorching.

serves 8 to 10
total time: 45 minutes

½ cup red wine vinegar

2 tablespoons whole-grain mustard

2 teaspoons sugar

Salt and pepper

2 shallots, halved through root end and sliced thin crosswise

8 slices bacon, cut into ½-inch pieces

2¼ pounds Brussels sprouts, trimmed, halved, and sliced thin

2¼ cups finely shredded radicchio, long strands cut into bite-size lengths

3 ounces Parmesan, shaved into thin strips using vegetable peeler

⅓ cup sliced almonds, toasted

1. Whisk vinegar, mustard, sugar, and ½ teaspoon salt together in bowl. Add shallots, cover tightly with plastic wrap, and microwave until steaming, 30 to 60 seconds. Stir briefly to submerge shallots. Cover and let cool to room temperature, 20 to 25 minutes.

2. Cook bacon in Dutch oven over medium heat, stirring frequently, until crisp and fat is rendered, 6 to 8 minutes. Off heat, whisk in shallot mixture. Add Brussels sprouts and radicchio and toss with tongs until dressing is evenly distributed and sprouts darken slightly, about 2 minutes. Transfer to serving bowl. Add Parmesan and almonds and toss to combine. Season with salt and pepper to taste, and serve immediately.

to make ahead
Shallot mixture, prepared through step 1, and prepped vegetables can be refrigerated separately for up to 24 hours. To serve, let shallot mixture come to room temperature, and continue with step 2.

baked goat cheese salad with pecans and radishes

why this recipe works Soft, creamy baked goat cheese over simple mixed greens makes for an enticing opening to a holiday meal, and our make ahead–friendly rendition of this restaurant standby could not be simpler to prepare. Giving the cheese a whirl in the food processor allowed us to incorporate fresh herbs for a subtle boost of flavor. For a little added flair, we coated the cheese rounds in chopped pecans rather than the usual bread crumbs, a swap that introduced appealing crunch and toasty, savory taste. Baking the frozen rounds in a blazing hot oven for just 7 to 10 minutes ensured a crisp coating and a smooth, but not quite melted, interior. Placed atop mixed greens tossed in a bright Dijon vinaigrette, this salad proved as easy as it was elegant. You can substitute walnuts, pistachios, or almonds for the pecans. Don't skimp on the goat cheese chilling times (in both steps 1 and 2) or the cheese will be very hard to work with.

serves 8
total time: 45 minutes
(plus 3 hours for chilling and freezing)

goat cheese
1½ cups pecans

12 ounces goat cheese, softened

2 tablespoons chopped fresh chives

1 teaspoon minced fresh thyme

2 large eggs

vinaigrette
5 teaspoons red wine vinegar

2 teaspoons Dijon mustard

1 small shallot, minced

⅛ teaspoon salt

Pinch pepper

¼ cup extra-virgin olive oil

Vegetable oil spray

12 ounces (12 cups) mesclun greens

4 radishes, trimmed and sliced thin

1. for the goat cheese Pulse pecans in food processor until finely chopped, about 15 pulses; transfer to bowl. Process goat cheese, chives, and thyme in food processor until smooth, about 30 seconds. Refrigerate cheese mixture in covered bowl until firm, about 1 hour.

2. Roll chilled cheese mixture into eight 1¾-inch balls (generous 2 tablespoons each). Beat eggs in medium bowl. Dip each cheese ball into eggs, then roll in chopped nuts, pressing gently to adhere. Arrange balls, 2 inches apart, on baking sheet and press into ¾-inch-thick rounds with greased bottom of dry measuring cup. Cover with plastic wrap and freeze until completely firm, at least 2 hours.

3. for the vinaigrette Whisk vinegar, mustard, shallot, salt, and pepper in small bowl. Whisking constantly, drizzle in oil.

4. Adjust oven rack to top position and heat oven to 475 degrees. Unwrap cheese and coat lightly with oil spray. Bake until nuts are golden brown and cheese is warmed through, 7 to 10 minutes.

5. In large bowl, gently toss mesclun greens with radishes. Whisk vinaigrette to re-emulsify, then drizzle over greens and toss gently to coat. Divide salad among 8 individual plates, top with warm goat cheese, and serve immediately.

to make ahead
Nut-crusted cheese balls can be frozen for up to 1 week in step 2. Vinaigrette can be refrigerated for up to 2 days. Let refrigerated vinaigrette sit at room temperature to allow oil to liquefy before beginning step 4.

centerpieces

roasted brined turkey

why this recipe works Brining brings out the best in roasted turkey: It helps the bird retain moisture, promises deep and thorough seasoning, and allows the meat to withstand high heat for appealingly crisp skin. After brining, we let the turkey dry in the refrigerator for optimal crisping. Brushing the skin with melted butter boosted its browning and added rich flavor to the finished turkey. To avoid overcooking the breast, we started out with the turkey placed breast side down in a V-rack and then rotated it after 45 minutes to an hour of roasting. This step kept the meat perfectly moist and juicy. Before carving, we let the turkey rest for at least 30 minutes to give the juices time to redistribute through the meat. We offer two brine formulas: one for a 4- to 6-hour brine and another for a 12- to 14-hour brine. If using a self-basting turkey (such as a frozen Butterball) or a kosher turkey, do not brine in step 1. If your turkey is large (18 to 22 pounds) and you are reluctant to rotate it in step 4, skip the step of lining the V-rack with foil and roast the bird breast-side up for the full time. See page 174 for carving instructions. Serve with Make-Ahead Turkey Gravy (page 47).

serves 10 to 22
total time: 1 hour 30 minutes
to 3 hours
(plus 12 hours 30 minutes
to 20 hours 45 minutes for
brining, chilling, and resting)

Salt

1 (12- to 22-pound) turkey, neck and giblets removed and reserved for gravy, if desired

4 tablespoons unsalted butter, melted

1. Dissolve 1 cup salt per gallon cold water for 4- to 6-hour brine or ½ cup salt per gallon cold water for 12- to 14-hour brine in large container. (For 12- to 17-pound turkey, use 2 gallons cold water; for 18- to 22-pound turkey, use 3 gallons cold water.) Submerge turkey in brine, cover, and refrigerate or store in very cool spot (40 degrees or less) for chosen brining time.

2. Remove turkey from brine and pat dry, inside and out, with paper towels. Place turkey on wire rack set in large rimmed baking sheet. Refrigerate, uncovered, for at least 8 to 24 hours.

3. Adjust oven rack to lowest position; heat oven to 400 degrees for 12- to 17-pound bird or 425 degrees for 18- to 22-pound bird. Line large V-rack with heavy-duty aluminum foil and poke several holes in foil; set V-rack in large roasting pan and spray foil with vegetable oil spray. Tie legs together using kitchen twine and tuck wings behind back. Brush breast with 2 tablespoons butter. Set turkey breast side down on prepared V-rack; brush back with remaining 2 tablespoons butter. Roast 45 minutes for 12- to 17-pound bird or 1 hour for 18- to 22-pound bird.

4. Remove roasting pan with turkey from oven (close oven door to retain oven heat); reduce oven temperature to 325 degrees if roasting 18- to 22-pound bird (do not change temperature for smaller bird). Using dish towels or 2 large wads of paper towels, rotate turkey breast side up. Continue to roast until breast registers 160 degrees and thighs register 175 degrees, 50 minutes to 1 hour longer for 12- to 14-pound bird, about 1¼ hours for 15- to 17-pound bird, or about 2 hours for 18- to 22-pound bird. Gently tip turkey up so that any accumulated juices in cavity run into roasting pan. Transfer turkey to carving board; let rest, uncovered, for 30 minutes (or up to 40 minutes for 18- to 22-pound bird). Carve and serve.

herbed roast turkey

why this recipe works The key to this boldly herbal turkey lies in infusing it with flavor at every level. An impactful herb paste rubbed on and beneath the skin got us on the right track, but slicing a pocket into each breast and filling them with the same paste put this bird's flavor over the top. If using a self-basting turkey (such as a frozen Butterball) or a kosher turkey, do not brine in step 1. For a turkey with extra-crisp skin, refrigerate, uncovered, for 8 to 24 hours in step 2. See page 172 for key prep instructions and page 174 for carving instructions. Serve with Make-Ahead Turkey Gravy (page 47).

serves 10 to 12
total time: 2 hours 30 minutes
(plus 5 hours for brining, chilling, and resting)

turkey and brine
2 cups salt

1 (12- to 14-pound) turkey, neck and giblets removed and reserved for gravy, if desired

herb paste
1¼ cups coarsely chopped fresh parsley

1 shallot, minced

4 teaspoons minced fresh thyme

2 garlic cloves, minced

2 teaspoons coarsely chopped fresh sage

1½ teaspoons minced fresh rosemary

¾ teaspoon grated lemon zest

¾ teaspoon salt

1 teaspoon pepper

¼ cup extra-virgin olive oil

1 teaspoon Dijon mustard

1. for the turkey and brine Dissolve salt in 2 gallons cold water in large container. Submerge turkey in brine, cover, and refrigerate or store in very cool spot (40 degrees or less) for 4 to 6 hours.

2. Remove turkey from brine and pat dry, inside and out, with paper towels. Place turkey, breast side up, on wire rack set in rimmed baking sheet and refrigerate, uncovered, for 30 minutes.

3. for the herb paste Pulse parsley, shallot, thyme, garlic, sage, rosemary, lemon zest, salt, and pepper in food processor until coarse paste is formed, 10 pulses. Add oil and mustard; continue to pulse until mixture forms smooth paste, 10 to 12 pulses; scrape sides of processor bowl with rubber spatula after 5 pulses. Transfer mixture to small bowl.

4. Adjust oven rack to lowest position and heat oven to 400 degrees. Line large V-rack with heavy-duty aluminum foil and poke several holes in foil. Set V-rack in large roasting pan and spray foil with vegetable oil spray.

5. Transfer turkey to large cutting board. Carefully loosen skin from meat of breast, thighs, and drumsticks. Using your fingers or spoon, slip 1½ tablespoons of paste under breast skin on each side of turkey. Using your fingers, distribute paste under skin over breast, thigh, and drumstick meat.

6. Using sharp paring knife, cut 1½-inch vertical slit into thickest part of each breast. Starting from top of incision, swing knife tip down to create 4- to 5-inch pocket within flesh. Place 1 tablespoon more paste in pocket of each breast; using your fingers, rub paste in thin, even layer.

7. Rub 1 tablespoon more paste inside turkey cavity. Rotate turkey breast side down; apply half of remaining herb paste to turkey skin; flip turkey breast side up and apply remaining herb paste to skin, pressing and patting to make paste adhere; reapply herb paste that falls onto cutting board. Tie legs together with kitchen twine and tuck wings behind back.

8. Place turkey, breast side down, on V-rack. Roast turkey for 45 minutes.

9. Remove pan from oven (close oven door to retain oven heat). Using dish towels or 2 large wads of paper towels, rotate turkey breast side up. Continue to roast until breast registers 160 degrees and thighs register 175 degrees, 50 minutes to 1 hour longer. Gently tip turkey up so that any accumulated juices in cavity run into roasting pan. Transfer turkey to a carving board and let rest, uncovered, for 30 minutes. Carve turkey and serve.

roast turkey for a crowd

why this recipe works Unless you have access to multiple ovens, only a very large turkey will do when you've got a crowd coming to dinner. But finding a container large enough to brine a gargantuan bird can be tricky, and turning the bird in the oven (our usual method for evenly cooked meat) can be tricky. We wanted the Norman Rockwell picture of perfection: a crisp, mahogany skin wrapped around tender, moist meat. And it had to be easy to prepare in a real home kitchen. We chose a Butterball turkey, which has already been brined for juicy flavor (a kosher bird, which has been salted, works well, too). A combination of high and low heat produced a tender, juicy bird with deeply browned skin. We boosted the savory flavor with the addition of onion, carrot, and celery, and a quartered lemon added bright, clean flavor. After roasting, we allowed the turkey to rest so the juices could redistribute. If you are reluctant to rotate the turkey in step 4, skip the step of lining the V-rack with foil and roast the bird breast side up for the full time. See page 174 for carving instructions. Serve with Make-Ahead Turkey Gravy (page 47).

serves 20 to 24
total time: 3 hours 30 minutes
(plus 30 minutes for resting)

3 onions, chopped coarse

3 carrots, chopped coarse

3 celery ribs, chopped coarse

1 lemon, quartered

2 sprigs fresh thyme

5 tablespoons unsalted butter, melted

1 (18- to 22-pound) turkey, neck and giblets removed and reserved for gravy, if desired

1 cup water, plus more as needed

1 teaspoon salt

1 teaspoon pepper

1. Adjust oven rack to lowest position. Heat oven to 425 degrees. Line large V-rack with heavy-duty foil and poke several holes in foil. Set V-rack in large roasting pan and spray foil with vegetable oil spray.

2. Toss half of onions, carrots, celery, lemon, and thyme with 1 tablespoon melted butter in medium bowl and place inside turkey. Tie legs together with kitchen twine and tuck wings behind back. Scatter remaining vegetables into roasting pan.

3. Pour 1 cup water over vegetable mixture. Brush turkey breast with 2 tablespoons melted butter, then sprinkle with half of salt and half of pepper. Place turkey, breast side down, on V-rack. Brush with remaining 2 tablespoons melted butter and sprinkle with remaining salt and pepper.

4. Roast turkey for 1 hour. Remove pan from oven; baste with juices from pan. Using dish towel or 2 large wads of paper towels, rotate turkey breast side up. If liquid in pan has totally evaporated, add another ½ cup water. Lower oven temperature to 325 degrees. Return turkey to oven and continue to roast until breast registers 160 degrees and thighs register 175 degrees, about 2 hours longer.

5. Remove turkey from oven. Gently tip turkey up so that any accumulated juices in cavity run into roasting pan. Transfer turkey to carving board. Let rest, uncovered, for 35 to 40 minutes. Carve turkey and serve.

braised turkey with gravy

why this recipe works The beauty of braising your holiday turkey is that it not only produces a perfectly cooked, ultraflavorful bird but also gives you the base for a robust built-in gravy. We worked with 10 pounds of turkey parts to maximize the meat's exposure to the cooking liquid, and a roomy roasting pan proved the perfect vessel for the job. By roasting the parts, chopped onions, celery, carrots, mushrooms, and garlic in a hot oven before adding the braising liquid, we were able to ensure plenty of browning, establishing a great deal of flavor from the get-go. Simmering the turkey in chicken broth cut with white wine infused the meat with savory, bright taste and got us on track for a standout gravy. All we had to do to finish it off was strain out the solids, build a roux using the liquid's skimmed fat, and simmer until the gravy reached the proper consistency. By the time the gravy was done, the turkey was ready to serve. If using self-basting or kosher turkey parts, do not brine in step 1, but do sprinkle with 1½ teaspoons salt.

serves 10 to 12
total time: 2 hours 45 minutes
(plus 3 hours for brining)

Salt and pepper

1 cup sugar

1 (5- to 7-pound) whole bone-in turkey breast, trimmed

4 pounds turkey drumsticks and thighs, trimmed

3 onions, chopped

3 celery ribs, chopped

2 carrots, peeled and chopped

½ ounce dried porcini mushrooms, rinsed

6 garlic cloves, crushed and peeled

6 sprigs fresh thyme

6 sprigs fresh parsley

2 bay leaves

4 tablespoons unsalted butter, melted

4 cups chicken broth

1 cup dry white wine

3 tablespoons all-purpose flour

1. Dissolve 1 cup salt and sugar in 2 gallons cold water in large container. Submerge turkey pieces in brine, cover, and refrigerate for at least 3 hours or up to 6 hours.

2. Adjust oven rack to lower-middle position and heat oven to 500 degrees. Remove turkey from brine and pat dry, inside and out, with paper towels. Toss onions, celery, carrots, mushrooms, garlic, thyme sprigs, parsley sprigs, bay leaves, and 2 tablespoons melted butter together in large roasting pan; arrange in even layer. Brush turkey pieces with remaining 2 tablespoons melted butter and season with pepper. Place turkey pieces, skin side up, on vegetables, leaving at least ¼ inch between pieces. Roast until skin is lightly browned, about 20 minutes.

3. Remove pan from oven and reduce temperature to 325 degrees. Pour broth and wine around turkey pieces (liquid should come about three-quarters up drumsticks and thighs). Place 16 by 12-inch piece of parchment paper over turkey pieces. Cover pan tightly with aluminum foil. Return

covered pan to oven and cook until breast registers 160 degrees and thighs register 175 degrees, 1¾ to 2¼ hours. Transfer turkey to carving board, tent with foil, and let rest for 20 minutes.

4. Strain vegetables and liquid from roasting pan through fine-mesh strainer set in large bowl; discard solids. Pour liquid into fat separator and let settle for 5 minutes. Reserve 3 tablespoons fat and 3 cups braising liquid.

5. Heat reserved fat in medium saucepan over medium-high heat. Add flour and cook, stirring constantly, until flour is dark golden brown and fragrant, about 5 minutes. Whisk in reserved braising liquid and bring to boil. Reduce heat to medium-low and simmer, stirring occasionally, until gravy is thick and reduced to 2 cups, 15 to 20 minutes. Remove gravy from heat and season with salt and pepper to taste.

6. Carve turkey and serve, passing gravy separately.

make-ahead roast turkey and gravy

why this recipe works What's the secret to roasting turkey ahead of time? Turkey parts. We first roasted a breast and legs in a V-rack over a pan filled with onions, carrots, celery, and garlic, using the vegetables for a rich make-ahead stock; we bolstered its flavor by roasting extra legs. The next day, we cut the breast from the bone and protected the delicate white meat by removing the skin, slicing the meat, and drizzling it with stock. Before reheating alongside the legs, we replaced the skin and wrapped the breast in foil. Enhanced turkey parts will work well here. If you prefer unenhanced parts, brine them, dissolving 1 cup of salt in 2 gallons of cold water, submerging the parts, covering, and refrigerating for 3 to 6 hours. Omit the salt in step 1.

serves 10 to 12
total time: 4 to 5 hours
(plus 5 hours for cooling and chilling)

2 onions, chopped

2 carrots, peeled and chopped

2 celery ribs, chopped

2 garlic cloves, peeled

2 teaspoons minced fresh thyme

4 (1½- to 1¾-pound) turkey leg quarters, trimmed

1 (6- to 7-pound) bone-in whole turkey breast, trimmed

4 tablespoons unsalted butter, melted

Salt and pepper

4 cups chicken broth

4 cups water

1 bay leaf

½ cup all-purpose flour

1. Adjust oven racks to middle and lowest positions and heat oven to 325 degrees. Place onions, carrots, celery, garlic, and thyme in large roasting pan. Set V-rack in pan. Pat turkey parts dry with paper towels. Arrange 2 legs and breast, skin side up, in V-rack. Evenly brush each piece with melted butter and season with salt and pepper. Place remaining 2 legs in 13 by 9-inch baking dish and season with salt and pepper.

2. Place pan on upper rack and dish on lower rack. Roast until breast registers 160 degrees and thighs register 175 degrees, 2 to 2½ hours. Transfer 2 legs and breast to wire rack set in rimmed baking sheet and let cool completely, about 2 hours.

3. Transfer vegetables and remaining 2 legs to large pot, scraping up any browned bits. Add broth, water, bay leaf, and 1 teaspoon pepper to pot and bring to boil. Reduce heat to low and simmer until reduced to 5 cups, 1¼ to 1½ hours.

4. Pour stock through fine-mesh strainer into large container; discard solids. Let cool for 1 hour, cover, and refrigerate for at least 4 hours or up to 2 days. Wrap cooled legs and breast tightly in plastic wrap and refrigerate for up to 2 days.

5. Scrape fat from top of chilled stock and reserve 5 tablespoons fat. Bring stock to simmer in medium saucepan over medium heat. Measure out and reserve ¼ cup stock.

6. Heat reserved fat in large saucepan over medium heat. Add flour and cook, whisking constantly, until golden, 3 to 4 minutes. Slowly whisk in remaining 4¾ cups stock and bring to boil. Reduce heat to medium-low and simmer until slightly thickened and reduced to 4 cups, 12 to 14 minutes. Season with salt and pepper to taste.

7. Meanwhile, adjust oven rack to middle position and heat oven to 500 degrees. Transfer legs and breast to carving board. Separate legs into thighs and drumsticks and arrange on wire rack set in rimmed baking sheet. Cut breast meat from bone into 2 single breasts. Working with 1 breast at a time, remove skin and set aside. Slice breast crosswise into ¼-inch-thick slices and place on 18 by 12-inch sheet of aluminum foil, keeping slices together. Pour 2 tablespoons reserved stock over breast and top with reserved skin. Wrap breast tightly and place on rack with legs.

8. Roast until meat is heated through and thighs and drumsticks are crispy, 20 to 25 minutes. Discard breast skin. Season with salt and pepper to taste. Serve, passing gravy separately.

one-pan roast turkey breast with herb stuffing

why this recipe works Serving a turkey breast is a great way to celebrate on a smaller scale, and this one-pan feast makes a festive, flavorful turkey dinner as foolproof as can be. To start, we sautéed fresh herbs and aromatics right in the roasting pan before placing an herb butter–rubbed turkey breast on top. There was plenty of room for a side in our roasting pan, so we worked in a stuffing, sprinkling bread cubes around the breast so they could toast in the oven while absorbing the turkey's flavorful juices. Starting at a high temperature allowed the juices to render for a supercrisp, deeply browned skin; we later lowered the heat to allow the breast to cook through gently. Served with our hands-off stuffing, this all-in-one meal kept things easy without shortchanging flavor. If using a self-basting turkey breast (such as a frozen Butterball) or kosher turkey, do not brine in step 1, but season with salt after rubbing with butter in step 2. Serve with Make-Ahead Turkey Gravy (page 47).

serves 4 to 6
total time: 2 hours 30 minutes
(plus 3 hours for brining)

Salt and pepper

1 (6- to 7-pound) bone-in whole turkey breast, trimmed

5 tablespoons unsalted butter, softened

2 tablespoons minced fresh sage

2 tablespoons minced fresh thyme

1 onion, chopped fine

2 celery ribs, minced

1 pound hearty white sandwich bread, cut into ½-inch cubes

1 cup chicken broth, plus extra as needed

1 tablespoon minced fresh parsley

1. Dissolve ½ cup salt in 1 gallon cold water in large container. Submerge turkey in brine, cover, and refrigerate for 3 to 6 hours; remove from brine and pat dry, inside and out, with paper towels.

2. Adjust oven rack to middle position and heat oven to 425 degrees. Mash 3 tablespoons butter, 1 tablespoon sage, 1 tablespoon thyme, 1 teaspoon salt, and ½ teaspoon pepper together in bowl. Using your fingers, gently separate skin from meat. Spread half of butter mixture under skin directly onto meat. Spread remaining butter mixture evenly over skin.

3. Melt remaining 2 tablespoons butter in large roasting pan over medium heat (over 2 burners, if possible). Add onion, celery, ¼ teaspoon salt, and ¼ teaspoon pepper and cook until vegetables are softened, about 5 minutes. Stir in remaining 1 tablespoon sage and remaining 1 tablespoon thyme and cook until fragrant, about 30 seconds. Off heat, place turkey, skin side up, on top of vegetables and arrange bread around turkey. Roast turkey for 30 minutes.

4. Reduce oven temperature to 325 degrees and continue to roast turkey until breast registers 160 degrees, about 1 hour.

5. Remove pan from oven. Transfer turkey to carving board, tent loosely with aluminum foil, and let rest 15 minutes. Stir broth and parsley into stuffing left in pan, cover with foil, and let stand 10 minutes; add extra broth if stuffing is dry. Carve turkey and serve with stuffing.

make-ahead turkey gravy

why this recipe works You can't serve turkey without gravy (and if you ask us, the same goes for mashed potatoes and stuffing, too), but this key part of any holiday feast is often left to the last minute, frantically cobbled together once the bird emerges from the oven. Our make-ahead gravy relieves some of the stress of holiday hosting and even boasts bigger turkey flavor than your typical gravy recipe. Good gravy comes from good stock, so we started by roasting turkey parts with chopped carrots, celery, onions, and garlic. Once the meat was deeply browned and the vegetables caramelized, we transferred everything to a Dutch oven. Chicken broth and white wine plus some sprigs of thyme promised flavorful, savory complexity. Following a lengthy simmer, we strained out the solids and proceeded with our gravy making (though the stock can be refrigerated or frozen for later use). We used the stock's fat to build a roux, browning a cup of flour in the heated fat before whisking in the stock. The finished gravy boasted all the body of a traditional preparation, but it was ready with time to spare and offered incredible meaty depth. If you wish to make this gravy at the same time as your turkey, you may add the giblets and neck along with the thighs or wings in step 1. Discard the strong-tasting liver before using the giblets. For more flavor, after roasting the turkey, skim the drippings from the pan and slowly add them to the gravy in step 4 (tasting as you go so the gravy does not become overly salty).

makes about 2 quarts
total time: 4 hours 30 minutes

6 turkey thighs, trimmed, or 9 wings, separated at the joints

Reserved turkey giblets and neck, optional

2 medium carrots, chopped coarse

2 medium celery ribs, chopped coarse

2 medium onions, chopped coarse

1 head garlic, halved

Vegetable oil spray

10 cups chicken broth, plus extra as needed

2 cups dry white wine

12 sprigs fresh thyme

Unsalted butter, as needed

1 cup all-purpose flour

Salt and pepper

Defatted turkey drippings, optional

1. Adjust oven rack to middle position and heat oven to 450 degrees. Toss thighs; giblets, if using; carrots; celery; onions; and garlic together in large roasting pan and spray with vegetable oil spray. Roast, stirring occasionally, until well browned, 1½ to 1¾ hours.

2. Transfer contents of roasting pan to Dutch oven. Add broth, wine, and thyme sprigs and bring to boil, skimming as needed. Reduce to gentle simmer and cook until broth is brown and flavorful and measures about 8 cups when strained, about 1½ hours. Strain broth through fine-mesh strainer into large container, pressing on solids to extract as much liquid as possible; discard solids.

3. Let strained turkey broth settle (if necessary), then spoon off and reserve ½ cup of fat that has risen to top (add butter as needed if short on turkey fat). Heat fat in Dutch oven over medium-high heat until bubbling. Whisk in flour and cook, whisking constantly, until well browned, 3 to 7 minutes.

4. Slowly whisk in turkey broth and bring to boil. Reduce to simmer and cook until gravy is very thick, 10 to 15 minutes. Add defatted drippings, if using, to taste, then season with salt and pepper to taste, and serve.

to make ahead
Following step 2, stock can be cooled and refrigerated for up to 2 days or frozen for up to 1 month. Gravy can be refrigerated for up to 2 days; reheat gently, adding additional chicken broth as needed to adjust consistency.

roasted cornish game hens

why this recipe works Quick-cooking roasted Cornish game hens are an easy, elegant dinner option, but achieving crisp, seasoned skin in the short cooking time can be a challenge. Poking holes in the skin helped the fat to render quickly, directing the fat away for quicker crisping. Baking powder is a proven browning agent, encouraging skin to take on rich color in no time, so we mixed it with oil and kosher salt and applied it to the hens' surfaces. To guarantee evenly cooked meat, we halved the small hens and started them out skin side down on a preheated baking sheet. We flipped them over for a final crisping stint under the broiler. This recipe requires refrigerating the salted hens for 4 to 24 hours before cooking (a longer salting time is preferable). If your hens weigh 1½ to 2 pounds, cook three instead of four, and extend the initial cooking time in step 5 to 15 minutes. We prefer Bell & Evans Cornish Game Hens. See page 172 for key prep instructions.

serves 4
total time: 45 minutes
(plus 4 hours for salting)

4 (1¼- to 1½-pound) Cornish game hens, giblets discarded

Kosher salt and pepper

¼ teaspoon vegetable oil

1 teaspoon baking powder

Vegetable oil spray

1. Using kitchen shears and working with 1 hen at a time, with hen breast side down, cut through bones on either side of backbone; discard backbone. Lay hens breast side up on counter. Using sharp chef's knife, cut through center of breast to make 2 halves.

2. Using your fingers, carefully separate skin from breasts and thighs. Using metal skewer or tip of paring knife, poke 10 to 15 holes in fat deposits on top of breasts and thighs. Tuck wingtips underneath hens. Pat hens dry with paper towels.

3. Sprinkle 1 tablespoon salt on underside (bone side) of hens. Combine 1 tablespoon salt and oil in small bowl and stir until salt is evenly coated with oil. Add baking powder and stir until well combined. Turn hens skin side up

and rub salt–baking powder mixture evenly over surface. Arrange hens skin side up and in single layer on large platter or plates and refrigerate, uncovered, for at least 4 hours or up to 24 hours.

4. Adjust oven racks to upper-middle and lower-middle positions, place rimmed baking sheet on lower rack, and heat oven to 500 degrees.

5. Once oven is fully heated, spray skin side of hens with oil spray and season with pepper. Carefully transfer hens, skin side down, to preheated sheet and cook for 10 minutes.

6. Remove hens from oven and heat broiler. Flip hens skin side up. Transfer sheet to upper rack and broil until well browned and breasts register 160 degrees and drumsticks/thighs register 175 degrees, about 5 minutes, rotating sheet as needed to promote even browning. Transfer to platter or individual plates and serve.

variations

herb-roasted cornish game hens
In step 3, combine 2 tablespoons salt with 1 teaspoon dried thyme,

1 teaspoon dried marjoram, and 1 teaspoon dried crushed rosemary. Sprinkle half of salt mixture on underside of hens; add oil to remaining salt-herb mixture until mixture is evenly coated with oil. Add baking powder to oil-salt mixture and proceed with recipe.

cumin-coriander roasted cornish game hens
In step 3, combine 2 tablespoons salt with 2 teaspoons ground cumin, 2 teaspoons ground coriander, 1 teaspoon paprika, and ¼ teaspoon cayenne pepper. Sprinkle half of salt mixture on underside of hens; add oil to remaining salt mixture until mixture is evenly coated with oil. Add baking powder to oil-salt mixture and proceed with recipe.

oregano-anise roasted cornish game hens
In step 3, combine 2 tablespoons salt with 1 teaspoon dried oregano, ½ teaspoon anise seeds, and ½ teaspoon hot smoked paprika Sprinkle half of salt mixture on underside of hens; add oil to remaining salt mixture until mixture is evenly coated with oil. Add baking powder to oil-salt mixture and proceed with recipe.

glazed spiral-sliced ham

why this recipe works Heating and glazing a cured ham seems effortless, but many recipes yield leathery meat in an overly sweet glaze. We wanted to guarantee moist meat in a nuanced glaze. Bone-in hams, labeled "with natural juices," have the best flavor, and spiral-sliced ones make carving a cinch, but too much time in the oven can ruin even the best ham on the market, so we focused on reducing the cooking time. Soaking the ham in hot water shaved off a full hour, and using an oven bag further reduced the cooking time while also containing the ham's moisture. We heated a mixture of sweet and savory pantry staples for two tempting glaze options. You may bypass the 1½-hour soaking time, but the ham will be less juicy and the heating time must increase to 18 to 20 minutes per pound. We prefer a tapered shank ham but a rounded sirloin ham will work here. If there is a tear or hole in the ham's inner covering, wrap it in several layers of plastic wrap before the hot-water soak. If you do not wish to use an oven bag, place the ham cut side down in the roasting pan and cover tightly with aluminum foil, adding 3 to 4 minutes per pound to the heating time.

serves 12 to 14
total time: 1 hour 45 minutes
(plus 1 hour 30 minutes
for soaking)

1 (7- to 10-pound) spiral-sliced bone-in half ham

1 large plastic oven bag

1 recipe glaze (recipes follow)

1. Leaving ham's inner plastic or foil covering intact, place ham in large container and cover with hot water; set aside for 45 minutes. Drain and cover again with hot water; set aside for another 45 minutes.

2. Adjust oven rack to lowest position and heat oven to 250 degrees. Unwrap ham; discard plastic disk covering bone. Place ham in oven bag. Gather top of bag tightly so bag fits snugly around ham, tie bag, and trim excess plastic. Set ham cut side down in large roasting pan and cut 4 slits in top of bag with knife.

3. Bake ham until center registers 100 degrees, 1 to 1½ hours (about 10 minutes per pound).

4. Remove ham from oven and increase oven temperature to 350 degrees. Cut open oven bag and roll back sides to expose ham. Brush ham with one-third of glaze and return to oven until glaze becomes sticky, about 10 minutes (if glaze is too thick to brush, return to heat to loosen).

5. Remove ham from oven, transfer to carving board, and brush entire ham with another third of glaze. Tent ham with aluminum foil and let rest for 15 minutes. While ham rests, add 4 to 6 tablespoons of ham juices to remaining one-third of glaze and cook over medium heat until thick but fluid sauce forms. Carve and serve ham, passing sauce separately.

cherry-port glaze
makes 1 cup

½ cup ruby port

½ cup cherry preserves

1 cup packed dark brown sugar

1 teaspoon pepper

Simmer port in small saucepan over medium heat until reduced to 2 tablespoons, about 5 minutes. Add remaining ingredients and cook, stirring occasionally, until reduced to 1 cup, 5 to 10 minutes; set aside.

maple-orange glaze
makes 1 cup

¾ cup maple syrup

½ cup orange marmalade

2 tablespoons unsalted butter

1 tablespoon Dijon mustard

1 teaspoon pepper

¼ teaspoon ground cinnamon

Combine ingredients in small saucepan and cook over medium heat, stirring occasionally, until reduced to 1 cup, 5 to 10 minutes; set aside.

slow-roasted fresh ham

why this recipe works Uncured, unsmoked, but capable of incredible meaty flavor, fresh ham is the perfect statement piece at the center of a rustic holiday meal. Because a standard brine does not make it very far into this hulking cut (and it's hard to find a container that can fit it), we seasoned the ham using a salt rub. Removing the thick skin and carving a crosshatch into the fat before applying a brown sugar–rosemary salt rub helped the seasoning really penetrate while also encouraging even rendering. Slicing a pocket into the ham's meaty end and filling it with the salt mixture also helped season the interior. After resting in the refrigerator for at least 12 hours, the ham was ready to roast. This cut stayed juicy during an extended roast thanks to the low oven temperature and the tight seal of an oven bag, and resting the ham in the bag allowed the ham to reabsorb any expelled moisture before serving. Our accompanying glaze came together in no time and gave this meaty ham an appealing finishing sheen. Use a turkey-size oven bag for this recipe. See page 172 for key prep instructions.

serves 12 to 14
total time: 4 hours 45 minutes
(plus 13 hours 15 minutes
for salting and resting)

1 (8- to 10-pound) bone-in, shank-end fresh ham

⅓ cup packed brown sugar

⅓ cup kosher salt

3 tablespoons minced fresh rosemary

1 tablespoon minced fresh thyme

1 large plastic oven bag

2 tablespoons maple syrup

2 tablespoons molasses

1 tablespoon soy sauce

1 tablespoon Dijon mustard

1 teaspoon pepper

1. Place ham flat side down on cutting board. Using sharp knife, remove skin, leaving ½- to ¼-inch layer of fat intact. Cut 1-inch diagonal crosshatch pattern in fat, being careful not to cut into meat. Place ham on its side. Cut one 4-inch horizontal pocket about 2 inches deep in center of flat side of ham, being careful not to poke through opposite side.

2. Combine sugar, salt, rosemary, and thyme in bowl. Rub half of sugar mixture in ham pocket. Tie 1 piece of kitchen twine tightly around base of ham. Rub exterior of ham with remaining sugar mixture. Wrap ham tightly in plastic wrap and refrigerate for at least 12 hours.

3. Adjust oven rack to lowest position and heat oven to 325 degrees. Set V-rack in large roasting pan. Unwrap ham and place in oven bag flat side down. Tie top of oven bag closed with kitchen twine. Place ham, flat side down, on V-rack and cut ½-inch slit in top of oven bag. Roast until meat, registers 160 degrees, 3½ to 5 hours. Remove ham from oven and let rest in oven bag on V-rack for 1 hour. Heat oven to 450 degrees.

4. Whisk maple syrup, molasses, soy sauce, mustard, and pepper together in bowl. Cut off top of oven bag and push down with tongs, allowing accumulated juices to spill into roasting pan; discard oven bag. Leave ham sitting flat side down on V-rack.

5. Brush ham with half of glaze and roast for 10 minutes. Brush ham with remaining glaze, rotate pan, and roast until deep amber color, about 10 minutes longer. Move ham to carving board, flat side down, and let rest for 20 minutes. Pour pan juices into fat separator. Carve ham into ¼-inch-thick slices, arrange on platter and moisten lightly with defatted pan juices. Serve, passing remaining pan juices separately.

to make ahead
Wrapped ham can be refrigerated for up to 24 hours following step 2.

crown roast of pork

why this recipe works A crown roast—two bone-in pork loin roasts tied together in a round—can feed a holiday crowd and offers a dramatic presentation, but its shape makes even cooking very challenging. Simply roasting it yields overcooked meat on the outside and undercooked meat around the inner circle. The solution? We turned the roast upside down to allow more air to circulate and to better expose the thickest part of the roast to the oven's heat. Beneath the pork we roasted small red potatoes, halved shallots, and apples. The apples softened and sopped up plenty of flavor, so we pureed them into a rich, fruity pan sauce. We served the roast with the potatoes and shallots piled into the center for an inviting presentation. Buy a pork loin roast with rib bones that have been trimmed clean, or "frenched." Check with the butcher that the chine bone has been cut from the crown roast; leaving this bone attached hinders even cooking. You want to buy the roast tied, but we tie it a second time for extra support. Use potatoes that measure 1 to 2 inches in diameter.

serves 10 to 12
total time: 2 hours
(plus 6 hours for salting)

Kosher salt and pepper

3 tablespoons minced fresh thyme

2 tablespoons minced fresh rosemary

5 garlic cloves, minced

1 (8- to 10-pound) pork crown roast (chine bone removed)

2 pounds small red potatoes

10 shallots, peeled and halved

2 Golden Delicious apples, peeled, cored, and halved

8 tablespoons unsalted butter, melted

½ cup apple cider

1 cup chicken broth

1. Combine 3 tablespoons salt, 1 tablespoon pepper, thyme, rosemary, and garlic in bowl; reserve 2 teaspoons for vegetables. Pat pork dry with paper towels and rub with remaining salt mixture. Wrap kitchen twine twice around widest part of roast and tie tightly. Refrigerate roast, covered, for at least 6 hours.

2. Adjust oven rack to lower-middle position and heat oven to 475 degrees. Place V-rack inside large roasting pan. Toss potatoes, shallots, apples, 4 tablespoons melted butter, and reserved 2 teaspoons herb salt together in large bowl and transfer to pan. Arrange roast bone side down in V-rack and brush with remaining 4 tablespoons melted butter. Roast until meat is well browned and registers 110 degrees, about 1 hour.

3. Remove roast from oven and reduce oven temperature to 300 degrees. Using 2 bunches of paper towels, flip roast bone side up. Add apple cider to pan and return to oven, rotating pan. Roast until meat registers 140 degrees, 30 to 50 minutes. Place meat on carving board, tent loosely with aluminum foil, and let rest for 15 to 20 minutes.

4. Transfer apple halves to blender and potatoes and shallots to bowl. Pour pan juices into fat separator, let liquid settle for 5 minutes, then pour into blender. Add broth to blender with apples and pan juices and process until smooth, about 1 minute. Transfer sauce to medium saucepan and bring to simmer over medium heat. Season with salt and pepper to taste. Cover and keep warm. Remove twine from roast, slice meat between bones, and serve with vegetables and sauce.

to make ahead
Covered roast can be refrigerated for up to 24 hours following step 1.

herb-stuffed pork loin

why this recipe works Mild in flavor and easy to infuse with big, bold taste, pork loin is the perfect starting place for a holiday-worthy roast. Butterflying and salting the pork promised deeply seasoned meat, and coating the interior with a Parmesan-herb paste gave it rich, Italian-inspired flavor. We rolled and tied the roast and gave it a quick stovetop sear for plenty of appealing browning. Roasting the pork in a low oven yielded a juicy interior beneath a mahogany crust, and the drippings made for an easy pan sauce. See page 173 for key prep instructions.

serves 8
total time: 2 hours 30 minutes
(plus 1 hour for salting)

1 (3- to 3½-pound) boneless center-cut pork loin roast

1 tablespoon packed brown sugar

Kosher salt and pepper

6 tablespoons extra-virgin olive oil

8 garlic cloves (3 sliced thin, 5 unpeeled)

2 ounces Parmesan cheese, grated (1 cup)

¾ cup minced fresh parsley

½ cup chopped fresh basil

¼ cup capers, minced

3 anchovy fillets, rinsed and minced

1 teaspoon grated lemon zest plus 2 teaspoons juice

1 shallot, peeled and halved

2 sprigs fresh rosemary

1½ tablespoons all-purpose flour

¼ cup dry white wine

2 cups chicken broth

¼ cup heavy cream

1. Position roast fat side up on cutting board. Insert knife two-thirds of the way up from bottom of roast along 1 long side and cut horizontally, stopping ½ inch before edge to create flap. Open up flap. At hinge, cut down into thicker portion of roast, stopping ½ inch from bottom. Pivot knife parallel to cutting board and cut horizontally in opposite direction, stopping ½ inch before edge, creating second flap. Open flap and lay meat flat. If meat is of uneven thickness, cover with plastic wrap and pound with meat pounder.

2. Combine sugar and 1 tablespoon salt in bowl. Sprinkle roast with sugar-salt mixture. Transfer roast to gallon-size zipper-lock bag, seal, and refrigerate for at least 1 hour.

3. Adjust oven rack to middle position and heat oven to 275 degrees. Heat ¼ cup oil and sliced garlic in ovensafe 12-inch nonstick skillet over medium-high heat until garlic begins to brown slightly, about 3 minutes. Transfer garlic and oil to bowl and let cool for 5 minutes. Stir Parmesan, parsley, basil, capers, anchovies, lemon zest, and ½ teaspoon pepper into garlic oil.

4. Place roast on cutting board, cut side up. Spread herb mixture evenly over surface of roast, leaving ½-inch border on all sides. Starting from short side farthest from exterior fat cap, roll tightly, then tie with kitchen twine at 1-inch intervals. Season roast with pepper.

5. Heat remaining 2 tablespoons oil in now-empty skillet over medium-high heat until just smoking. Brown roast on all sides, about 10 minutes. Flip roast seam side down in skillet. Add shallot, rosemary sprigs, and unpeeled garlic cloves to skillet and transfer to oven. Cook until thickest part of roast registers 135 degrees, 1 hour 5 minutes to 1 hour 10 minutes. Transfer roast to carving board, tent with aluminum foil, and let rest for 30 minutes. Do not clean skillet.

6. Meanwhile, use spoon to smash garlic in skillet (skillet handle will be hot). Place skillet over medium-high heat and cook until shallot and garlic are sizzling. Stir in flour and cook, stirring, for 1 minute. Add wine and cook until nearly evaporated, about 2 minutes. Add broth and cream and bring to boil. Reduce heat to medium-low and simmer until sauce is reduced to about 1 cup and thickened, 10 to 12 minutes. Strain through fine-mesh strainer set over small saucepan; discard solids. Stir in lemon juice. Season with salt and pepper to taste. Cover and keep warm.

7. Discard twine, slice roast ½ inch thick, and serve, passing sauce separately.

to make ahead
The roast can be refrigerated for up to 24 hours following step 2.

porchetta

why this recipe works Pork butt is an indulgent cut that turns ultra-tender through slow roasting. Inspired by Italy's favorite street food—a crackling-skinned roast hog—we reimagined *porchetta* for the holiday table. To infuse the meat with porchetta's hallmark herbal flavor and to impart a crust reminiscent of the crispy hog skin, we carved a crosshatch into the fat cap and applied a paste of fennel seeds, rosemary, thyme, and garlic. Halving the hefty cut and cooking it low and slow promised two evenly cooked roasts in less time; a direct blast of heat at the end delivered a burnished exterior. Pork butt is often labeled Boston butt or Boston shoulder. Look for a roast with a substantial fat cap. If fennel seeds are unavailable, substitute ¼ cup of ground fennel. See page 173 for key prep instructions.

serves 3 to 10
total time: 3 hours 15 minutes
(plus 6 hours for salting
and resting)

3 tablespoons fennel seeds

½ cup fresh rosemary leaves (2 bunches)

¼ cup fresh thyme leaves (2 bunches)

12 garlic cloves, peeled

Kosher salt and pepper

½ cup extra-virgin olive oil

1 (5- to 6-pound) boneless pork butt roast, trimmed

¼ teaspoon baking soda

1. Grind fennel seeds in spice grinder or mortar and pestle until finely ground. Transfer ground fennel to food processor and add rosemary, thyme, garlic, 1 tablespoon pepper, and 2 teaspoons salt. Pulse mixture until finely chopped, 10 to 15 pulses. Add oil and process until smooth paste forms, 20 to 30 seconds.

2. Using sharp knife, cut slits in surface fat of roast, spaced 1 inch apart, in crosshatch pattern, being careful not to cut into meat. Cut roast in half with grain into 2 equal pieces.

3. Turn each roast on its side so fat cap is facing away from you,

bottom of roast is facing toward you, and newly cut side is facing up. Starting 1 inch from short end of each roast, use boning or paring knife to make slit that starts 1 inch from top of roast and ends 1 inch from bottom, pushing knife completely through roast. Repeat making slits, spaced 1 to 1½ inches apart, along length of each roast, stopping 1 inch from opposite end (you should have 6 to 8 slits, depending on size of roast).

4. Turn roast so fat cap is facing down. Rub sides and bottom of each roast with 2 teaspoons salt, taking care to work salt into slits from both sides. Rub herb paste onto sides and bottom of each roast, taking care to work paste into slits from both sides. Flip roast so that fat cap is facing up. Using 3 pieces of kitchen twine per roast, tie each roast into compact cylinder.

5. Combine 1 tablespoon salt, 1 teaspoon pepper, and baking soda in small bowl. Rub fat cap of each roast with salt–baking soda mixture, taking care to work mixture into crosshatches. Transfer roasts to wire rack set in rimmed baking sheet and refrigerate, uncovered, for at least 6 hours or up to 24 hours.

6. Adjust oven rack to middle position and heat oven to 325 degrees. Transfer roasts, fat side up, to large roasting pan, leaving at least 2 inches between roasts. Cover tightly with aluminum foil. Cook until pork registers 180 degrees, 2 to 2½ hours.

7. Remove pan from oven and increase oven temperature to 500 degrees. Carefully remove and discard foil and transfer roasts to large plate. Discard liquid in pan. Line pan with foil. Remove twine from roasts; return roasts to pan, directly on foil; and return pan to oven. Cook until exteriors of roasts are well browned and interiors register 190 degrees, 20 to 30 minutes.

8. Transfer roasts to carving board and let rest for 20 minutes. Slice roasts ½ inch thick, transfer to serving platter, and serve.

to make ahead
The porchetta needs to be refrigerated for 6 to 24 hours once it is rubbed with the paste, but it is best when it sits for a full 24 hours.

onion-braised beef brisket

why this recipe works A slow braise in a rich onion sauce and an overnight rest to absorb the sauce's flavors turn this brisket meltingly tender. This recipe requires extended unattended cooking and advance preparation. Defatting the sauce is essential. For a spicy sauce, use ¼ teaspoon of cayenne pepper. You will need 18-inch-wide heavy-duty aluminum foil for this recipe.

serves 6 to 8
total time: 5 to 6 hours
(plus overnight soaking)

1 (4- to 5-pound) beef brisket, flat cut, fat trimmed to ¼ inch

Salt and pepper

1 teaspoon vegetable oil, plus extra as needed

2½ pounds onions, halved and sliced ½ inch thick

1 tablespoon packed brown sugar

3 garlic cloves, minced

1 tablespoon tomato paste

1 tablespoon paprika

⅛ teaspoon cayenne pepper

2 tablespoons all-purpose flour

1 cup chicken broth

1 cup dry red wine

3 bay leaves

3 sprigs fresh thyme

2 teaspoons cider vinegar

1. Adjust oven rack to lower-middle position and heat oven to 300 degrees. Line 13 by 9-inch baking dish with two 24-inch-long sheets of 18-inch-wide heavy-duty aluminum foil, placing sheets perpendicular to each other and allowing foil to extend beyond edges of pan. Pat brisket dry with paper towels. Place brisket, fat side up, on carving board; using fork, poke holes in meat through fat layer about 1 inch apart. Season both sides with salt and pepper.

2. Heat oil in 12-inch skillet over medium-high heat until oil just begins to smoke. Place brisket, fat side up, in skillet (brisket may climb up sides of pan); weight brisket with heavy Dutch oven or cast-iron skillet and cook until well browned, about 7 minutes. Remove Dutch oven; using tongs, flip brisket and cook on second side without weight until well browned, about 7 minutes longer. Transfer brisket to platter.

3. Pour off all but 1 tablespoon fat from pan (or add enough oil to fat in skillet to equal 1 tablespoon); stir in onions, sugar, and ¼ teaspoon salt and cook over medium-high heat, stirring occasionally, until onions are softened, 10 to 12 minutes. Add garlic and cook, stirring frequently, until fragrant, about 1 minute; add tomato paste and cook, stirring to combine, until paste darkens, about 2 minutes. Add paprika and cayenne and cook, stirring constantly, until fragrant, about 1 minute. Add flour and cook, stirring constantly, until well combined, about 2 minutes. Add broth, wine, bay leaves, and thyme sprigs, stirring to scrape up browned bits from pan; bring to simmer and simmer for 5 minutes.

4. Pour sauce and onions into foil-lined baking dish. Nestle brisket, fat side up, in sauce and onions. Fold foil extensions over and seal (do not tightly crimp foil because foil must later be opened to test for doneness). Place in oven and cook until fork slips easily into meat, 3 to 4 hours (when testing for doneness, open foil carefully, as contents will be steaming). Carefully open foil and let brisket cool at room temperature, 20 to 30 minutes.

5. Transfer brisket to large bowl; set fine-mesh strainer over bowl and strain sauce over brisket. Discard bay leaves and thyme sprigs from onions and transfer onions to small bowl. Cover both bowls with plastic wrap, cut vents in plastic, and refrigerate overnight.

6. About 45 minutes before serving, adjust oven rack to lower-middle position; heat oven to 350 degrees. Transfer cold brisket to carving board. Scrape off and discard fat from surface of sauce, then heat sauce in medium saucepan over medium heat until warm, skimming any fat on surface with wide shallow spoon (you should have about 2 cups sauce without onions; if necessary, simmer over medium-high heat until reduced to 2 cups). Slice brisket against grain into ¼-inch-thick slices and place slices in 13 by 9-inch baking dish. Stir reserved onions and vinegar into warmed sauce and season with salt and pepper to taste. Pour sauce over brisket, cover baking dish with foil, and bake until heated through, 25 to 30 minutes. Serve immediately.

roast beef tenderloin

why this recipe works With its uniformly rosy, luxuriously tender meat beneath a deeply browned crust, it's hard to top beef tenderloin for a special occasion. Though this premium cut is easy to prepare, its meek flavor requires a little help. After salting the roast for thorough seasoning, we gently roasted it in a low oven and gave it a good sear at the end. To bring a little more richness to the table, we pulled together a simple but impactful flavored butter, rubbed it over the hot roast, and saved some extra for serving time. Ask your butcher to prepare a trimmed center-cut Châteaubriand from the whole tenderloin, as this cut is not usually available without special ordering. If you are cooking for a crowd, this recipe can be doubled to make two roasts. Sear the roasts one after the other, wiping out the pan and adding new oil after searing the first roast. Both pieces of meat can be roasted on the same rack.

serves 4 to 6
total time: 1 hour 15 minutes
(plus 1 hour for salting)

1 (2-pound) beef tenderloin center-cut Châteaubriand, trimmed

2 teaspoons kosher salt

1 teaspoon coarsely ground pepper

2 tablespoons unsalted butter, softened

1 tablespoon vegetable oil

1 recipe flavored butter (recipes follow)

1. Using 12-inch lengths of kitchen twine, tie roast crosswise at 1½-inch intervals. Sprinkle roast evenly with salt, cover loosely with plastic wrap, and let stand at room temperature for 1 hour. Meanwhile, adjust oven rack to middle position and heat oven to 300 degrees.

2. Pat roast dry with paper towels. Sprinkle roast evenly with pepper and spread butter evenly over surface. Transfer roast to wire rack set in rimmed baking sheet. Roast until center of roast registers 125 degrees (for medium-rare),

40 to 55 minutes, or 135 degrees (for medium), 55 minutes to 1 hour 10 minutes, flipping roast halfway through cooking.

3. Heat oil in 12-inch skillet over medium-high heat until just smoking. Place roast in skillet and sear until well browned on all sides, 1 to 2 minutes per side. Transfer roast to carving board and spread 2 tablespoons flavored butter evenly over top of roast; let rest for 15 minutes. Remove twine and cut meat crosswise into ½-inch-thick slices. Serve, passing remaining flavored butter separately.

shallot and parsley butter
makes about ½ cup

4 tablespoons unsalted butter, softened

1 small shallot, minced

1 tablespoon finely chopped fresh parsley

1 garlic clove, minced

¼ teaspoon salt

¼ teaspoon pepper

Combine all ingredients in medium bowl.

chipotle and garlic butter with lime and cilantro
makes about ½ cup

5 tablespoons unsalted butter, softened

1 medium chipotle chile in adobo sauce, seeded and minced, with 1 teaspoon adobo sauce

1 tablespoon minced fresh cilantro

1 garlic clove, minced

1 teaspoon honey

1 teaspoon grated lime zest

½ teaspoon salt

Combine all ingredients in medium bowl.

boneless rib roast with yorkshire pudding

why this recipe works Richly marbled and great for feeding a crowd, juicy boneless rib roast is a British holiday favorite, often served with meaty jus and slices of custardy golden Yorkshire pudding to sop everything up. If you're using a dark roasting pan, reduce the pudding's cooking time by 5 minutes. See page 173 for key prep instructions. Serve with Horseradish Sauce.

serves 8 to 10
total time: 4 hours
(plus 24 hours for salting)

roast and pudding

1 (5- to 5½-pound) first-cut boneless beef rib roast with ½-inch fat cap

Kosher salt and pepper

2½ cups (12½ ounces) all-purpose flour

4 cups milk

4 large eggs

1 tablespoon vegetable oil, plus extra as needed

jus

1 onion, chopped fine

1 teaspoon cornstarch

2½ cups beef broth

1 sprig fresh thyme

1. for the roast and pudding Using sharp knife, trim roast's fat cap to ¼-inch thickness; refrigerate trimmings. Cut 1-inch crosshatch pattern in fat cap, being careful not to cut into meat. Rub 2 tablespoons salt over entire roast and into crosshatch. Transfer to large plate and refrigerate, uncovered, for at least 24 hours.

2. Adjust oven rack to lower-middle position and heat oven to 250 degrees. Spray roasting pan with vegetable oil spray. Cut reserved trimmings into ½-inch pieces. Place 3 ounces (about ¾ cup) trimmings in bottom of pan. Set V-rack over trimmings in pan.

3. Season roast with pepper and place fat side up on V-rack. Roast until meat registers 115 degrees (for rare), 120 degrees (for medium-rare), or 125 degrees (for medium), 2½ to 3 hours.

4. Meanwhile, combine flour and 1 tablespoon salt in large bowl. Whisk milk and eggs in second bowl until fully combined. Slowly whisk milk mixture into flour mixture until smooth. Cover with plastic wrap and let rest at room temperature for 1 hour.

5. Transfer V-rack with roast to carving board, tent with aluminum foil, and let rest for 1 hour. Using fork, remove solids in pan, leaving liquid fat behind (there should be about 6 tablespoons; if not, supplement with extra vegetable oil). Increase oven temperature to 425 degrees.

6. When oven reaches 425 degrees, return pan to oven and heat until fat is just smoking, 3 to 5 minutes. Rewhisk batter and pour into center of pan. Bake until pudding is dark golden brown and edges are crisp, 40 to 45 minutes.

7. Meanwhile, pat roast dry with paper towels. Heat 1 tablespoon oil in 12-inch skillet over medium-high heat until just smoking. Sear roast on all sides until evenly browned, 5 to 7 minutes. Transfer roast to carving board.

8. for the jus Return skillet to medium-high heat and add onion. Cook until onion is just softened, about 3 minutes, scraping up any browned bits. Whisk cornstarch into broth. Add broth mixture and thyme sprig to skillet and bring to boil. Reduce heat to medium-low and simmer until reduced by half, about 7 minutes. Strain jus through fine-mesh strainer set over small saucepan; discard solids. Cover and keep warm.

9. Slice roast ¾ inch thick. Cut pudding into squares in pan. Serve with pudding and jus.

horseradish sauce
makes about 1 cup
Buy refrigerated prepared horseradish, not the shelf-stable kind.

½ cup sour cream

½ cup prepared horseradish

1½ teaspoons kosher salt

⅛ teaspoon pepper

Combine all ingredients in bowl. Refrigerate for at least 30 minutes.

to make ahead
Roast can be refrigerated for up to 4 days in step 1. Batter can be refrigerated for up to 24 hours; let come to room temperature before proceeding. Horseradish Sauce can be refrigerated for up to 2 days.

roast butterflied leg of lamb
with cumin and mustard seeds

why this recipe works Butterflied leg of lamb is an intimidating cut to work with due to its bulking size and irregular shape. Pounding the meat to even thickness not only tamed it into a much simpler cut to cook, but ensured maximum juicy meat and crisp crust. A spiced oil seasoned the meat and made for an easy sauce. We prefer the subtler flavor of domestic lamb. The 2 tablespoons of salt in step 1 is for a 6-pound leg. Add a teaspoon of salt for every additional pound if you use a larger leg.

serves 8 to 10
total time: 2 hours 30 minutes

lamb
1 (6- to 8-pound) butterflied leg of lamb

Kosher salt

⅓ cup vegetable oil

3 shallots, sliced thin

4 garlic cloves, peeled and smashed

1 (1-inch) piece ginger, sliced into ½-inch-thick rounds and smashed

1 tablespoon coriander seeds

1 tablespoon cumin seeds

1 tablespoon mustard seeds

3 bay leaves 2 (2-inch) strips lemon zest

sauce
⅓ cup chopped fresh mint

⅓ cup chopped fresh cilantro

1 shallot, minced

2 tablespoons lemon juice

Salt and pepper

1. for the lamb Place lamb on cutting board with fat cap facing down. Using sharp knife, trim any pockets of fat and connective tissue from underside of lamb. Flip lamb over, trim fat cap so it's between ⅛ and ¼ inch thick, and pound roast to even 1-inch thickness. Cut slits, spaced ½ inch apart, in fat cap in crosshatch pattern, being careful to cut down to but not into meat. Rub 2 tablespoons salt over entire roast and into slits. Let stand, uncovered, at room temperature for 1 hour.

2. Meanwhile, adjust 1 oven rack to lower-middle position and second rack 4 to 5 inches from broiler element and heat oven to 250 degrees. Stir together oil, shallots, garlic, ginger, coriander seeds, cumin seeds, mustard seeds, bay leaves, and lemon zest on rimmed baking sheet and bake on lower-middle rack until spices are softened and fragrant and shallots and garlic turn golden, about 1 hour. Remove sheet from oven and discard bay leaves.

3. Thoroughly pat lamb dry with paper towels and transfer, fat side up, to sheet (directly on top of spices). Roast on lower rack until lamb registers 120 degrees, 30 to 40 minutes. Remove sheet from oven and heat broiler. Broil lamb on upper rack until surface is well browned and charred in spots and lamb registers 125 degrees (for medium-rare), 3 to 8 minutes.

4. Remove sheet from oven and, using 2 pairs of tongs, transfer lamb to carving board (some spices will cling to bottom of roast); tent with aluminum foil and let rest for 20 minutes.

5. for the sauce Meanwhile, carefully pour pan juices through fine-mesh strainer into medium bowl, pressing on solids to extract as much liquid as possible; discard solids. Stir in mint, cilantro, shallot, and lemon juice. Add any accumulated lamb juices to sauce and season with salt and pepper to taste.

6. With long side facing you, slice lamb with grain into 3 equal pieces. Turn each piece and slice across grain into ¼-inch-thick slices. Serve with sauce. (Briefly warm sauce in microwave if it has cooled and thickened.)

variations

roast butterflied leg of lamb
with rosemary and red pepper
Omit cumin and mustard seeds. Toss 6 sprigs fresh rosemary and ½ teaspoon red pepper flakes with oil mixture in step 2. Substitute parsley for cilantro in sauce.

roast butterflied leg of lamb
with fennel and black pepper
Substitute 1 tablespoon fennel seeds for cumin seeds and 1 tablespoon black peppercorns for mustard seeds in step 2. Substitute parsley for mint in sauce.

roasted rack of lamb

why this recipe works Roasting a rack of lamb is a simple process, but there's a fine line between a showstopper and a dried-out disappointment. For a rack that would do us proud at our next fête, we sough spot-on seasoning, juicy meat, and a bold relish to serve alongside it. Carving a shallow cross-hatch into the fat cap and rubbing the racks' surfaces with a blend of kosher salt and ground cumin loaded the lamb with flavor. Roasting the meat was as simple as arranging the lamb on a wire rack set in a baking sheet. While the racks roasted, we pulled together a punchy accompanying relish, combining chopped roasted red pepper, minced parsley, olive oil, fresh lemon juice, and garlic. To give the racks a flavorful brown crust, we seared them in a skillet before serving. We prefer the milder taste and bigger size of domestic lamb, but you may substitute lamb imported from New Zealand or Australia. Since imported racks are generally smaller, in step 1 season each rack with ½ teaspoon of the salt mixture and cook for 50 minutes to 1 hour 10 minutes.

serves 4 to 6
total time: 1 hour 45 minutes

lamb
2 (1¾- to 2-pound) racks of lamb, fat trimmed to ⅛ to ¼ inch and rib bones frenched

Kosher salt

1 teaspoon ground cumin

1 teaspoon vegetable oil

relish
½ cup jarred roasted red peppers, rinsed, patted dry, and chopped fine

½ cup minced fresh parsley

¼ cup extra-virgin olive oil

¼ teaspoon lemon juice

⅛ teaspoon garlic, minced to paste

Kosher salt and pepper

1. for the lamb Adjust oven rack to middle position and heat oven to 250 degrees. Using sharp knife, cut slits in fat cap, spaced ½ inch apart, in crosshatch pattern (cut down to, but not into, meat). Combine 2 tablespoons salt and cumin in bowl. Rub ¾ teaspoon salt mixture over entire surface of each rack and into slits. Reserve remaining salt mixture. Place racks, bone side down, on wire rack set in rimmed baking sheet. Roast until meat registers 125 degrees (for medium-rare) or 130 degrees (for medium), 1 hour 5 minutes to 1 hour 25 minutes.

2. for the relish While lamb roasts, combine red peppers, parsley, olive oil, lemon juice, and garlic in bowl. Season with salt and pepper to taste. Let stand at room temperature for at least 1 hour before serving.

3. Heat vegetable oil in 12-inch skillet over high heat until just smoking. Place 1 rack, bone side up, in skillet and cook until well browned, 1 to 2 minutes. Transfer to carving board. Pour off all but 1 teaspoon fat from skillet and

repeat browning with second rack. Tent racks with aluminum foil and let rest for 20 minutes. Cut between ribs to separate chops and sprinkle cut side of chops with ½ teaspoon salt mixture. Serve, passing relish and remaining salt mixture separately.

variation
roasted rack of lamb with sweet mint-almond relish
Substitute ground anise for cumin in salt mixture. Omit red pepper relish. While lamb roasts, combine ½ cup minced fresh mint; ¼ cup sliced almonds, toasted and chopped fine; ¼ cup extra-virgin olive oil; 2 tablespoons red currant jelly; 4 teaspoons red wine vinegar; and 2 teaspoons Dijon mustard in bowl. Season with salt and pepper to taste. Let stand at room temperature for at least 1 hour before serving.

to make ahead
Relish can be refrigerated for up to 2 days. Let refrigerated relish sit at room temperature for at least 1 hour before serving.

pan-seared duck breasts with dried cherry sauce

why this recipe works With rich, tender meat and impossibly crispy skin, seared duck breasts make any dinner special. Duck breasts cooked over high heat turned a deep mahogany brown quickly, but the fat had no time to render before it came time to flip them. By adopting a more gradual approach, heating a dry skillet over medium to build up some heat before dropping it to medium-low and adding the duck breasts, skin side down, we were able to render the fat completely while the skin turned a deep golden brown. Once flipped, the breasts needed just 2 to 5 minutes to finish cooking to a juicy medium-rare. The accompanying sweet-tart sauce came together effortlessly: Starting with some of the rendered duck fat, we softened minced shallots and added in dried cherries, reducing red wine and chicken broth in turns to finish. A pat of butter and some lemon juice gave our sauce a rich, bright finish. Cooking the duck skin side down over moderate heat is key to properly render the fat and crisp the skin; adjust the stove temperature as needed to maintain a constant but gentle simmer during this cooking time. Both a traditional and nonstick skillet will work here, but a nonstick skillet makes for easier cleanup. We prefer to cook duck breasts to medium-rare; however, you can cook them to your desired level of doneness in step 2.

serves 4
total time: 1 hour

4 boneless duck breast halves (about 6 ounces each), skin scored on diagonal

Salt and pepper

2 shallots, minced

¾ cup dry red wine

¼ cup dried cherries

1 cup chicken broth

2 tablespoons unsalted butter

1 teaspoon lemon juice

1. Pat duck breasts dry with paper towels and season with salt and pepper. Heat 12-inch nonstick skillet over medium heat until hot, about 3 minutes. Add duck breasts, skin side down, lower heat to medium-low, and cook until fat begins to render, about 5 minutes. Continue to cook, adjusting heat as needed for fat to maintain constant but gentle simmer, until most of fat has rendered and skin is deep golden and crisp, 20 to 25 minutes longer.

2. Flip duck breasts over and continue to cook until center of breasts register 125 degrees (for medium-rare), 2 to 5 minutes. Transfer duck to cutting board, tent with foil, and let rest while making sauce (duck temperature will rise to 130 degrees before serving).

3. Pour off all but 1 tablespoon fat from skillet. Add shallots and cook over medium-high heat until softened, 2 to 3 minutes. Add wine and dried cherries and cook until liquid has reduced to syrupy consistency, about 4 minutes. Add chicken broth and cook until sauce has thickened and measures about 1 cup, about 5 minutes. Whisk in butter and remove skillet from heat. Stir in lemon juice and season with salt and pepper to taste. Slice duck breasts thin and serve, passing sauce separately.

variation

pan-seared duck breasts with green peppercorn sauce Substitute ruby port for red wine and 2 tablespoons crushed dried green peppercorns for dried cherries. Add ½ cup heavy cream with chicken broth and omit butter in step 3.

oven-poached side of salmon

why this recipe works A poached side of salmon is an elegant choice when entertaining, but we wanted to employ this method of cooking without a poacher. Fortunately, this proved as easy as steaming the salmon right in its own moisture. We wrapped the seasoned fish in foil and placed it directly on the oven rack, which offered more even cooking than using a baking sheet. Cooking the salmon low and slow yielded the best results—moist, rich fish that we paired with a fresh, flavorful relish. If serving a big crowd, you can oven-poach two individually wrapped sides of salmon in the same oven (on the upper- and lower-middle racks) without altering the cooking time. White wine vinegar can be substituted for the cider vinegar.

serves 8 to 10
total time: 1 hour
(plus 1 hour 30 minutes
for cooling and chilling)

1 (4-pound) skin-on side of salmon, pinbones removed

Salt

2 tablespoons cider vinegar

6 sprigs fresh tarragon or dill, plus 2 tablespoons minced

2 lemons, sliced thin, plus wedges for serving

1. Adjust oven rack to middle position and heat oven to 250 degrees. Cut 3 pieces of heavy-duty aluminum foil to be 1 foot longer than side of salmon. Working with 2 pieces of foil, fold up 1 long side of each by 3 inches. Lay sheets side by side with folded sides touching, fold edges together to create secure seam, and press seam flat. Center third sheet of foil over seam. Spray foil with vegetable oil spray.

2. Pat salmon dry with paper towels and season with salt. Lay salmon, skin side down, in center of foil. Sprinkle with vinegar, then top with tarragon sprigs and lemon slices. Fold foil up over salmon to create seam on top and gently fold foil edges together to secure; do not crimp too tightly.

3. Lay foil-wrapped fish directly on oven rack (without baking sheet). Cook until color of salmon has turned from pink to orange and thickest part registers 135 to 140 degrees, 45 minutes to 1 hour.

4. Remove fish from oven and open foil. Let salmon cool at room temperature for 30 minutes. Pour off any accumulated liquid, then reseal salmon in foil and refrigerate until cold, at least 1 hour.

5. Unwrap salmon and brush away lemon slices, tarragon sprigs, and any solidified poaching liquid. Transfer fish to serving platter, sprinkle with minced tarragon, and serve with lemon wedges.

grapefruit and basil relish
makes about 1 cup
The sweetness of this relish depends on the sweetness of the grapefruits. If the grapefruits are sour, add a pinch of sugar to the relish.

2 ruby red grapefruits, peeled, segmented, and cut into ½-inch pieces

2 tablespoons chopped fresh basil

1 small shallot, minced

2 teaspoons lemon juice

2 teaspoons extra-virgin olive oil

Salt and pepper

Place grapefruits in strainer set over bowl and let drain for 15 minutes; reserve 1 tablespoon drained juice. Combine reserved juice, basil, shallot, lemon juice, and oil in bowl. Stir in drained grapefruits and let sit for 15 minutes. Season with salt and pepper to taste.

fresh tomato relish
makes about 1 cup
Use very ripe tomatoes in this simple relish.

2 tomatoes, cored, seeded, and cut into ¼-inch pieces

1 small shallot, minced

1 small garlic clove, minced

2 tablespoons chopped fresh basil

1 tablespoon extra-virgin olive oil

1 teaspoon red wine vinegar

Salt and pepper

Combine all ingredients in bowl, let sit for 15 minutes, and season with salt and pepper to taste.

to make ahead
Salmon can be refrigerated for up to 2 days in step 4. Let sit at room temperature for 30 minutes before serving.

lobster fettuccine with fennel and tarragon

why this recipe works Dotted with tender bites of lobster and infused with the sweet anise notes of fennel and tarragon, this luxuriously creamy pasta dish truly sets the tone for an elegant celebration. We began by softening onion and fennel in olive oil before blooming thyme, garlic, and cayenne for a complexly flavored base. We built the sauce from there, adding a hit of dry sherry, chicken broth, and cream, plus some water to keep it from turning overly rich. After cooking the pasta in the simmering sauce, we added generous chunks of cooked lobster, allowing them to warm through before serving. Stirring in tarragon at the end kept its flavor fresh, and lemon juice offered a bright finish. You can purchase cooked lobster meat or steam and shell lobsters yourself following the instructions below. Use dried fettuccine in this recipe; fresh fettuccine will not work. When adding the fettuccine in step 2, stir gently to avoid breaking the noodles; they will soon soften enough to allow for easier stirring. Serve the pasta as soon as it is finished; the sauce will turn thick and clumpy if held for too long. Serving bowls warmed in a 200-degree oven will help extend the serving time for the pasta. You will need at least a 6-quart Dutch oven for this recipe.

serves 8 to 10
total time: 45 minutes

3 tablespoons olive oil

1 onion, chopped fine

1 fennel bulb, stalks discarded, bulb halved, cored, and chopped fine

Salt and pepper

1 tablespoon minced fresh thyme

3 garlic cloves, minced

¼ teaspoon cayenne pepper

¾ cup dry sherry

4 cups chicken broth

4 cups water

2 cups heavy cream

2 pounds fettuccine

2 pounds cooked lobster meat, cut into ⅓-inch pieces

3 tablespoons minced fresh tarragon

1 tablespoon lemon juice

Grated Parmesan cheese

1. Heat oil in large Dutch oven over medium heat until shimmering. Add onion, fennel, and ½ teaspoon salt and cook until softened, 5 to 7 minutes. Stir in thyme, garlic, and cayenne and cook until fragrant, about 30 seconds. Stir in sherry and simmer until it has nearly evaporated, about 4 minutes.

2. Stir in broth, water, cream, and pasta. Increase heat to medium-high and cook at vigorous simmer, stirring often, until pasta is tender and sauce has thickened, 12 to 15 minutes.

3. Reduce heat to low and add lobster and tarragon. Cook, gently tossing to combine, until lobster is just warmed through, about 3 minutes. Off heat, stir in lemon juice and season with salt and pepper to taste. Serve in warm bowls with Parmesan.

steamed lobster
Fit Dutch oven with steamer basket and fill with water until water just touches bottom of basket; bring to boil over high heat. Add the lobsters, cover, and steam according to the times in chart (see page 174), checking pot periodically and adding water as needed. Let lobsters cool slightly before shelling them.

to make ahead
Cooked lobster meat can be refrigerated for up to 2 days.

vegetable moussaka

why this recipe works Traditional *moussaka* pairs eggplant and generously spiced ground meat in a fragrant, rich sauce. For an impressive vegetarian interpretation that maintains this dish's warming, rustic characteristics, we used bulgur and potatoes to establish a hearty foundation. Blooming cinnamon with sautéed onion and garlic built great flavor, and simmering the potatoes before baking ensured they would turn out tender. Bulgur only requires a soak to soften up, so we simply stirred it into the potato-tomato mixture and let it absorb the surrounding liquid (and all the rich flavor that came with it). We readied the eggplant layer by roasting bite-size pieces, concentrating their flavor. A thick béchamel spread over the top before baking made for a rich, bubbly cap to this hearty dish. When buying eggplant, look for those that are glossy, feel firm, and are heavy for their size. You can swap fine-grind bulgur for the medium-grind in this recipe. Do not substitute low-fat or skim milk in the sauce.

serves 6 to 8
total time: 2 hours

4 pounds eggplant, peeled and cut into ¾-inch pieces

¼ cup extra-virgin olive oil

Salt and pepper

1 onion, chopped fine

4 garlic cloves, minced

1 tablespoon minced fresh oregano or 1 teaspoon dried

1 teaspoon ground cinnamon

½ cup dry white wine

1 pound russet potatoes, peeled and cut into ½-inch pieces

2 cups vegetable broth

1 (28-ounce) can crushed tomatoes

1 cup medium-grind bulgur, rinsed

3 tablespoons unsalted butter

¼ cup all-purpose flour

2 cups whole milk

2 ounces Parmesan cheese, grated (1 cup)

Pinch ground nutmeg

2 tablespoons chopped fresh basil

1. Adjust oven racks to upper-middle and lower-middle positions and heat oven to 450 degrees. Line 2 rimmed baking sheets with aluminum foil and spray with vegetable oil spray. Toss eggplant with 3 tablespoons oil, 1 teaspoon salt, and ¼ teaspoon pepper and spread evenly over prepared sheets. Bake until eggplant is light golden brown and tender, 40 to 50 minutes, switching and rotating sheets halfway through roasting. Set eggplant aside to cool. Reduce oven temperature to 400 degrees and adjust oven rack to middle position.

2. Meanwhile, heat remaining 1 tablespoon oil in Dutch oven over medium heat until shimmering. Add onion and ½ teaspoon salt and cook until onion is softened, about 5 minutes. Stir in garlic, oregano, and cinnamon and cook until fragrant, about 30 seconds. Stir in wine, scraping up any browned bits, until nearly all liquid is evaporated, about 2 minutes. Stir in potatoes and broth and bring to simmer. Cover, reduce heat to low, and cook until potatoes are nearly tender, about 15 minutes.

3. Stir in tomatoes and their juice and cook, uncovered, until flavors meld, about 5 minutes. Off heat, stir in bulgur and let sit until grains are tender and most of liquid is absorbed, about 15 minutes. Transfer to 13 by 9-inch baking dish and top evenly with roasted eggplant to form compact layer.

4. Melt butter in now-empty pot over medium heat. Stir in flour and cook for 1 minute. Gradually whisk in milk, bring to simmer, and cook, whisking often, until sauce thickens and no longer tastes of flour, about 5 minutes. Off heat, whisk in Parmesan and nutmeg and season with salt and pepper to taste. Pour sauce over eggplant and smooth into even layer.

5. Cover with foil and bake until bubbling around edges, about 15 minutes. Uncover and continue to bake until top is light golden brown around edges, about 15 minutes. Let cool for 10 minutes. Sprinkle with basil and serve.

fennel, olive, and goat cheese tarts

why this recipe works These Mediterranean-inspired tarts are an elegant yet easy vegetarian option to add to your holiday table. We used convenient store-bought puff pastry for the tart crust to keep the recipe simple and fuss-free. The combination of fennel's fresh anise flavor and the briny bite of cured olives made for a bold filling. Tangy goat cheese thinned with olive oil and brightened with fresh basil offered a pleasant contrast to the rich, flaky pastry and helped bind the vegetables and pastry together. We par-baked the pastry on its own, allowing it to puff up nicely before the filling was added. To keep the fennel, olives, and goat cheese firmly in place, we cut a border around the edges of the baked crusts and lightly pressed down on the centers to make neat beds for the cheese and vegetables. Just 5 minutes more in the oven heated the filling through and browned the crusts beautifully. To thaw frozen puff pastry, let it sit either in the refrigerator for 24 hours or on the counter for 30 minutes to 1 hour.

serves 4
total time: 45 minutes

1 (9½ by 9-inch) sheet puff pastry, thawed and cut in half

3 tablespoons extra-virgin olive oil

1 large fennel bulb, stalks discarded, bulb halved, cored, and sliced thin

3 garlic cloves, minced

½ cup dry white wine

½ cup pitted oil-cured black olives, chopped

1 teaspoon grated lemon zest plus 1 tablespoon juice

Salt and pepper

8 ounces goat cheese, softened

5 tablespoons chopped fresh basil

1. Adjust oven rack to middle position and heat oven to 425 degrees. Lay puff pastry halves on parchment paper–lined baking sheet and poke all over with fork. Bake pastry until puffed and golden brown, about 15 minutes, rotating baking sheet halfway through baking. Using tip of paring knife, cut ½-inch-wide border around top edge of each pastry, then press centers down with your fingertips.

2. Meanwhile, heat 1 tablespoon oil in 12-inch skillet over medium-high heat until shimmering. Add fennel and cook until softened and browned, about 10 minutes. Stir in garlic and cook until fragrant, 30 seconds. Add wine, cover, and cook for 5 minutes. Uncover and cook until liquid has evaporated and fennel is very soft, 3 to 5 minutes. Off heat, stir in olives and lemon juice and season with salt and pepper to taste.

3. Mix goat cheese, ¼ cup basil, remaining 2 tablespoons oil, lemon zest, and ¼ teaspoon pepper together in bowl, then spread evenly over center of pastry shells. Spoon fennel mixture over top.

4. Bake tarts until cheese is heated through and crust is deep golden, 5 to 7 minutes. Sprinkle with remaining 1 tablespoon basil and serve.

variation
artichoke, shallot, and goat cheese tarts
Substitute one 9-ounce box frozen artichoke hearts, thawed and patted dry, for fennel. Add 1 shallot, halved and sliced thin, and ½ teaspoon salt to skillet with artichokes; cook until artichokes are tender and spotty brown, 3 to 5 minutes. After adding wine, do not cover skillet. Cook until wine evaporates, about 3 minutes. Omit olives and lemon zest. Substitute 2 teaspoons balsamic vinegar for lemon juice.

to make ahead
Filled tarts can be held at room temperature for 2 hours following step 3.

mushroom lasagna

why this recipe works This lasagna brings meaty, earthy depth to the table, making it perfect for any cold-weather celebration. We unlocked the deep flavors of everyday mushrooms, layered them with no-boil noodles, and united the dish with béchamel sauce and cheese. A garlic-herb topping offered a fresh finish. Whole-milk mozzarella can be used in place of fontina cheese.

serves 8 to 10
total time: 2 hours

2 pounds portobello mushroom caps, gills removed, halved and sliced crosswise ¼ inch thick

¼ cup extra-virgin olive oil

Salt and pepper

4 red onions, chopped

8 ounces white mushrooms, trimmed and halved if small or quartered if large

½ ounce dried porcini mushrooms, rinsed and minced

4 garlic cloves, minced

½ cup dry vermouth

3 tablespoons unsalted butter

3 tablespoons all-purpose flour

1 cup water

3½ cups whole milk

¼ teaspoon ground nutmeg

¼ cup plus 2 tablespoons chopped fresh basil

¼ cup minced fresh parsley

12 no-boil lasagna noodles

8 ounces Italian fontina cheese, shredded (2 cups)

1½ ounces Parmesan cheese, grated (¾ cup)

½ teaspoon grated lemon zest

1. Adjust oven rack to middle position and heat oven to 425 degrees. Toss portobello mushrooms with 2 tablespoons oil, ½ teaspoon salt, and ½ teaspoon pepper and spread onto rimmed baking sheet. Roast until shriveled, about 30 minutes, stirring halfway through roasting; transfer to bowl and let cool.

2. Meanwhile, heat 1 tablespoon oil in 12-inch nonstick skillet over medium heat until shimmering. Add onions, ¼ teaspoon salt, and ¼ teaspoon pepper and cook, stirring occasionally, until onions are softened and lightly browned, 8 to 10 minutes; transfer to bowl with roasted portobellos.

3. Pulse white mushrooms in food processor until coarsely chopped, about 6 pulses. Heat remaining 1 tablespoon oil in now-empty skillet over medium-high heat until shimmering. Add chopped mushrooms and porcini and cook, stirring occasionally, until browned and all moisture has evaporated, 6 to 8 minutes. Stir in 1 tablespoon garlic, 1 teaspoon salt, and 1 teaspoon pepper, reduce heat to medium, and cook, stirring often, until garlic is fragrant, about 30 seconds. Stir in vermouth and cook until liquid has evaporated, 2 to 3 minutes.

4. Add butter and cook until melted. Add flour and cook, stirring constantly, for 1 minute. Stir in water, scraping up any browned bits. Stir in milk and nutmeg and simmer until sauce has thickened and measures 4 cups, 10 to 15 minutes. Off heat, stir in ¼ cup basil and 2 tablespoons parsley.

5. Pour 2 inches boiling water into 13 by 9-inch baking dish. Add noodles one at a time and soak until pliable, about 5 minutes, separating noodles with tip of sharp knife to prevent sticking. Remove noodles from water and place in single layer on clean dish towels; discard water. Dry and grease dish.

6. Combine fontina and Parmesan in bowl. Spread 1 cup mushroom sauce evenly over bottom of prepared dish. Arrange 3 noodles in single layer on top of sauce. Spread ¾ cup sauce evenly over noodles, then sprinkle with 2 cups mushroom-onion mixture and ¾ cup cheese mixture. Repeat layering of noodles, mushroom sauce, mushroom-onion mixture, and cheese mixture 2 more times. Arrange remaining 3 noodles on top, cover with remaining sauce, and sprinkle with remaining cheese.

7. Cover dish tightly with aluminum foil that has been sprayed with vegetable oil spray and bake until edges are just bubbling, about 20 minutes, rotating dish halfway through baking. Remove foil, increase oven temperature to 500 degrees, and continue to bake until cheese on top becomes spotty brown, 6 to 8 minutes.

8. Combine remaining garlic, remaining 2 tablespoons basil, remaining 2 tablespoons parsley, and lemon zest together and sprinkle over lasagna. Let cool for 15 minutes before serving.

shareable sides

whipped potatoes

why this recipe works These whipped potatoes yield the lightest, most ethereally fluffy side of spuds you've ever tasted, making them perfect for pairing with all of your holiday favorites. We rinsed the potatoes before cooking to remove their surface starch, the main culprit behind gummy mashed potatoes. Steaming—rather than boiling—the potatoes kept them from absorbing extra liquid. A quick toss in the pot dried the potatoes further, so that they whipped up to maximum fluffiness in the mixer. Since the texture of the potatoes was already creamy, we used a mixture of melted butter and whole milk, rather than heavy cream, to moisten and flavor the potatoes. Do not attempt to cook the potatoes in a pot smaller than 12 quarts; if you don't have a large enough pot, use two smaller pots and cook the potatoes in two simultaneous batches. If your steamer basket has short legs (under 1¾ inches), the potatoes will sit in water as they cook and get wet. To prevent this, use balls of aluminum foil as steamer basket stilts. A stand mixer fitted with a whisk attachment yields the smoothest potatoes, but you can also use a handheld mixer and a large bowl.

serves 12
total time: 45 minutes

6 pounds russet potatoes, peeled and cut into 1-inch pieces

2 cups whole milk

12 tablespoons unsalted butter, cut into pieces

2 teaspoons salt

¾ teaspoon pepper

1. Rinse potatoes in colander under cold water until water runs clear, about 1 minute; drain well. Fill 12-quart Dutch oven with 1 inch water and bring to boil. Place steamer basket in pot, add potatoes, and cover. Reduce heat to medium and cook until potatoes are tender, 25 to 30 minutes.

2. Meanwhile, heat milk, butter, salt, and pepper in small saucepan over medium-low heat, whisking until smooth, about 3 minutes; cover and keep warm.

3. Carefully pour potatoes into colander, drain well, then return to pot. Cook over low heat, stirring constantly, until potatoes are thoroughly dried, about 1 minute.

4. Using stand mixer fitted with whisk attachment, whip half of potatoes into small pieces on low speed, about 30 seconds. Add half of milk mixture in steady stream until incorporated. Increase speed to high and whip until potatoes are light and fluffy and no lumps remain, about 2 minutes, scraping down bowl as needed. Transfer to large, warm serving bowl and cover to keep warm. Repeat with remaining potatoes and milk mixture. Serve.

to make ahead
Peeled and cut potatoes can be refrigerated, submerged in water, for up to 24 hours. Drain potatoes before proceeding with recipe. Whipped potatoes, covered, can be held at room temperature for up to 20 minutes.

garlic mashed potatoes

why this recipe works Mashed potatoes infused with roasted garlic flavor makes for an indulgent side, and this streamlined version delivers the deep flavor and aroma of slow-roasted garlic with less fuss by cooking the garlic directly with the potatoes. To eliminate excess starch, which produced gluey mashed potatoes, we gave raw, cut russets a thorough rinse before adding them to the pot. After cooking plenty of minced garlic (with sugar to mimic the sweetness roasting imparts), we added the potatoes and simmered them in butter and some half-and-half—just enough liquid to prevent scorching. Cutting the potatoes into ½-inch pieces ensured that maximum surface area was exposed to soak up garlicky flavor.

serves 8 to 10
total time: 45 minutes

4 pounds russet potatoes, peeled, quartered, and cut into ½-inch pieces

12 tablespoons unsalted butter, cut into 12 pieces

12 garlic cloves, minced

1 teaspoon sugar

1½ cups half-and-half

½ cup water

Salt and pepper

1. Place cut potatoes in colander. Rinse under cold running water until water runs clear, about 1 minute; drain thoroughly.

2. Melt 4 tablespoons butter in Dutch oven over medium heat. Cook garlic and sugar, stirring often, until sticky and straw colored, 3 to 4 minutes. Add rinsed potatoes, 1¼ cups half-and-half, water, and 1 teaspoon salt to pot and stir to combine. Bring to boil, then reduce heat to low and simmer, covered and stirring occasionally, until potatoes are tender and most of the liquid is absorbed, 25 to 30 minutes.

3. Off heat, add remaining 8 tablespoons butter to pot and mash with potato masher until smooth. Using rubber spatula, fold in remaining ¼ cup half-and-half until liquid is absorbed and potatoes are creamy. Season with salt and pepper. Serve.

to make ahead
Peeled and cut potatoes can be refrigerated, submerged in water, for up to 24 hours. Drain potatoes before proceeding with recipe. Mashed potatoes, covered, can be held at room temperature for up to 20 minutes.

scalloped potatoes

why this recipe works In our experience, most recipes for scalloped potatoes take hours of work yet still produce unevenly cooked potatoes in a heavy, curdled sauce. This version is faster than most and produces layer upon layer of thinly sliced, tender potatoes, creamy sauce, and nicely browned, cheesy crust. Simmering the potatoes briefly in heavy cream thinned out with milk before moving the production into a baking dish cut the cooking time significantly while also eliminating the risk of raw potatoes in the finished dish. A sprinkling of cheddar cheese and a mere 20 minutes in the oven were enough to produce an appealingly browned, cheesy crust. Russet potatoes, thinly sliced, gave us neat layers with the best texture and flavor. For the fastest and most consistent results, slice the potatoes in a food processor.

serves 8 to 10
total time: 1 hour

2 tablespoons unsalted butter

1 small onion, chopped fine

2 cloves garlic, minced

4 pounds russet potatoes, peeled and cut into ⅛-inch-thick slices

3 cups heavy cream

1 cup whole milk

4 sprigs fresh thyme

2 bay leaves

2 teaspoons salt

½ teaspoon pepper

4 ounces cheddar cheese, shredded (about 1 cup)

1. Heat oven to 350 degrees. Melt butter in large Dutch oven over medium-high heat. Add onion and sauté until it turns soft and begins to brown, about 4 minutes. Add garlic and sauté until fragrant, about 30 seconds. Add potatoes, cream, milk, thyme sprigs, bay leaves, salt, and pepper and bring to simmer. Cover, adjusting heat as necessary to maintain light simmer, and cook until potatoes are almost tender (paring knife can be slipped into and out of center of potato slice with some resistance), about 15 minutes.

2. Discard thyme sprigs and bay leaves. Transfer potato mixture to 3-quart baking dish and sprinkle with cheese. Bake until cream has thickened and is bubbling around sides and top is golden brown, about 20 minutes. Let cool for 5 minutes before serving.

to make ahead
Do not top casserole with cheddar; casserole can be refrigerated for up to 24 hours. To serve, cover dish tightly with greased aluminum foil and bake in 400-degree oven until hot throughout, about 1 hour. Uncover, top with cheddar, and continue to bake until cheddar is lightly browned, about 30 minutes. Let casserole cool for 15 minutes before serving.

baked macaroni and cheese

why this recipe works A Southern holiday staple, our cheesy, velvety, bubbling baked macaroni and cheese pairs with all of our favorite holiday dishes. To turn out a perfectly cooked casserole void of dry pasta or curdled sauce, we cooked the pasta until just past al dente and then combined it with a lush béchamel-based cheese sauce, turning to garlic, dry mustard, and cayenne for complexity and chicken broth for deeply savory flavor. For maximum cheesiness and a creamy texture, we used both sharp cheddar and Colby cheeses. As soon as the pasta and sauce had heated through on the stovetop we transferred the macaroni to a baking dish, sprinkled the surface with toasty Parmesan bread crumbs, and baked it long enough to heat through and build some appealing browning. Although the classic pasta shape for this dish is elbow macaroni, any small, curvaceous pasta will work. It's crucial to cook the pasta until tender—that is, just past the al dente stage. Whole, low-fat, and skim milk all work well in this recipe. The recipe may be halved and baked in an 8-inch square, broiler-safe baking dish. If desired, offer celery salt or hot sauce for sprinkling at the table.

serves 10 to 12, or 6 to 8 as a main
total time: 1 hour 15 minutes

6 slices hearty white sandwich bread, torn into quarters

3 tablespoons unsalted butter, cut into 6 pieces and chilled, plus 5 tablespoons unsalted butter

1 pound elbow macaroni

Salt and pepper

1 garlic clove, minced

1 teaspoon dry mustard

¼ teaspoon cayenne pepper

6 tablespoons all-purpose flour

2¼ cups chicken broth

3½ cups whole milk

1 pound Colby cheese, shredded (about 4 cups)

8 ounces extra-sharp cheddar cheese, shredded (about 2 cups)

1. Adjust oven rack to lower-middle position and heat oven to 400 degrees. Pulse bread and chilled butter in food processor until coarsely ground, 10 to 15 pulses; set aside.

2. Bring 4 quarts water to boil in Dutch oven over high heat. Add macaroni and 1 tablespoon salt and cook, stirring occasionally, until tender, about 5 minutes. Drain the pasta and leave it in the colander; set aside.

3. Melt remaining butter in now-empty pot over medium-high heat. Stir in garlic, mustard, and cayenne and cook until fragrant, about 30 seconds. Stir in flour and cook, stirring constantly, until golden, about 1 minute. Slowly whisk in chicken broth and milk. Bring to a simmer and cook, whisking often, until large bubbles form on surface and mixture is slightly thickened, about 15 minutes. Off heat, gradually whisk in cheeses until completely melted. Season with salt and pepper to taste.

4. Stir drained pasta into cheese sauce, breaking up any clumps, until well combined. Pour into 13 by 9-inch baking dish and sprinkle with crumb topping. Bake macaroni until sauce is bubbling and crumbs are crisp, 25 to 35 minutes.

to make ahead
Do not heat oven in step 1. Following sprinkling of bread crumbs in step 4, wrap macaroni tightly with plastic wrap and then foil and refrigerate for up to 2 days or freeze for up to 1 month. (If frozen allow to thaw completely in refrigerator for 24 hours.) To reheat, unwrap dish and cover tightly with aluminum foil. Bake until filling is hot throughout, 40 to 45 minutes. Remove foil and continue to bake until crumbs are crisp 15 to 20 minutes longer.

pureed butternut squash

why this recipe works With its silky-smooth texture and earthy, lightly sweetened flavor, pureed butternut squash is a serious crowd-pleaser. This version offers some improvements to the traditional protocol, wherein tender cooked squash is pureed with butter and heavy cream in a food processor. After testing a variety of cooking methods for the squash, we discovered that microwaving worked best; not only was it easy, but this method also produced clean squash flavor and encouraged the squash to shed as much as a cup of liquid, concentrating its sweet flavor in no time. (The liquid had a slightly bitter flavor, so we left it out of the puree.) Whirred in the food processor with a hit of half-and-half and a few pats of butter, this squash puree emerged smooth and lush with a touch of richness. Aside from some brown sugar, salt, and pepper, we kept the flavoring simple, allowing the star ingredient to shine. You can substitute delicata squash for the butternut squash.

serves 8 to 10
total time: 30 minutes

2 medium butternut squash (about 4 pounds), peeled, seeded, and cut into 1½-inch chunks

¼ cup half-and-half

4 tablespoons unsalted butter

2 tablespoons brown sugar, plus extra as needed

Salt and pepper

1. Microwave squash in covered bowl until tender and easily pierced with fork, 15 to 20 minutes, stirring squash halfway through cooking time.

2. Drain squash in colander, then transfer to food processor. Add half-and-half, butter, 2 table-spoons brown sugar, and 1 teaspoon salt. Process until smooth, about 20 seconds, stopping to scrape down bowl as needed.

3. Transfer pureed squash to serving dish and season with salt, pepper, and additional sugar to taste. Serve.

variations
pureed butternut squash with sage and toasted almonds
While squash cooks in microwave, cook 2 tablespoons butter with 1 teaspoon minced fresh sage in small skillet over medium-low heat until fragrant, about 2 minutes. Substitute sage butter for butter added to food processor in step 2. Sprinkle with ½ cup toasted sliced almonds before serving.

pureed butternut squash with orange
Follow recipe for Pureed Butternut Squash, adding 4 tablespoons orange marmalade to food processor with butter in step 2.

pureed butternut squash with honey and chipotle chile
Substitute honey for sugar. Add 1 tablespoon minced canned chipotle chile in adobo sauce to food processor with butter in step 2.

to make ahead
Add only 2 tablespoons butter in step 2. Following step 2, puree can be refrigerated for up to 4 days, or frozen for up to 1 month. (If frozen, thaw completely in refrigerator for 24 hours before reheating.) Transfer the cold puree to a microwave-safe bowl, cover, and microwave on high power, stirring occasionally, until hot, 3 to 5 minutes. Stir in remaining 2 tablespoons butter, and season with additional sugar, salt, and pepper to taste.

roasted butternut squash with goat cheese, pecans, and maple

why this recipe works Butternut squash is put through the recipe wringer every autumn, so we sought to create a savory recipe for roasted squash that was simple yet stately, whether as a colorful side or a full-flavored vegetarian main. Peeling the squash removed not only the tough outer skin but also the rugged fibrous layer of white flesh just beneath, ensuring supremely tender squash. To encourage the squash slices to caramelize, we cranked the oven to 425 degrees, tossed the squash in melted butter, placed the slices on the lowest rack, and baked them long enough to evaporate their water. For toppings that added crunch, creaminess, and a little sweetness, we picked pecans, goat cheese, and maple syrup spiked with cayenne. This dish can be served warm or at room temperature. For the best texture, be sure to peel the squash thoroughly, removing all of the fibrous flesh just below the squash's skin.

serves 4 to 6
total time: 1 hour 30 minutes

2½–3 pounds butternut squash

3 tablespoons unsalted butter, melted

½ teaspoon salt

½ teaspoon pepper

2 tablespoons maple syrup

Pinch cayenne pepper

1½ ounces goat cheese, crumbled (⅓ cup)

⅓ cup pecans, toasted and chopped coarse

2 teaspoons fresh thyme leaves

1. Adjust oven rack to lowest position and heat oven to 425 degrees. Using sharp vegetable peeler or chef's knife, remove skin and fibrous threads just below skin from squash (squash should be completely orange, with no white flesh). Halve squash lengthwise and scrape out seeds. Place squash, cut side down, on cutting board and slice crosswise into ½-inch-thick pieces.

2. Toss squash with melted butter, salt, and pepper and arrange on rimmed baking sheet in single layer. Roast squash until side touching sheet toward back of oven is well browned, 25 to 30 minutes. Rotate sheet and continue to bake until side touching sheet toward back of oven is well browned, 6 to 10 minutes.

3. Remove squash from oven and use metal spatula to flip each piece. Continue to roast until squash is very tender and side touching sheet is browned, 10 to 15 minutes.

4. Transfer squash to platter. Combine maple syrup and cayenne in bowl, then drizzle over squash. Sprinkle squash with goat cheese, pecans, and thyme and serve.

variations

roasted butternut squash with radicchio and parmesan
Omit maple syrup and cayenne. Whisk 1 tablespoon sherry vinegar, ½ teaspoon mayonnaise, and pinch salt together in bowl. Gradually whisk in 2 tablespoons extra-virgin olive oil until smooth; drizzle over cooked squash. Substitute ½ ounce Parmesan, shaved into thin strips, for goat cheese 3 tablespoons toasted pine nuts for pecans, and ½ cup coarsely shredded radicchio for thyme.

roasted butternut squash with tahini and feta
Omit maple syrup and cayenne. Whisk 1 tablespoon tahini, 1 tablespoon extra-virgin olive oil, 1½ teaspoons lemon juice, 1 teaspoon honey, and pinch salt together in bowl; drizzle over cooked squash. Substitute ¼ cup finely crumbled feta cheese for goat cheese, ¼ cup toasted and finely chopped pistachios for pecans, and 2 tablespoons chopped fresh mint for thyme.

candied sweet potato casserole

why this recipe works Sweet potato casserole is a must-have side on many Thanksgiving tables, but this dish often takes a hard turn at "candied" and becomes overly saccharine. For a casserole with restrained, sophisticated sweetness, we set out to incorporate a more savory accent. For optimum soft texture and nuanced flavor, we steamed the sweet potatoes on the stovetop with butter and brown sugar. We kept the other flavors simple—just salt and pepper. For the candied topping, we used whole pecans instead of chopped; this gave the casserole a better texture and striking rustic appearance. Tossing the nuts with beaten egg white, brown sugar, and a little cayenne and cumin ensured a balanced pecan topping with an inviting sheen and some welcome contrasting heat. For a more intense molasses flavor, use dark brown sugar in place of light.

serves 10 to 12
total time: 1 hour 45 minutes

sweet potatoes
8 tablespoons unsalted butter, cut into 1-inch chunks

5 pounds sweet potatoes (about 8 medium), peeled and cut into 1-inch cubes

1 cup packed light brown sugar

½ cup water

1½ teaspoons salt

½ teaspoon pepper

pecan topping
2 cups pecans

½ cup packed light brown sugar

1 egg white, lightly beaten

⅛ teaspoon salt

Pinch cayenne pepper

Pinch ground cumin

1. for the sweet potatoes Melt butter in Dutch oven over medium-high heat. Add sweet potatoes, sugar, water, salt, and black pepper; bring to simmer. Reduce heat to medium-low, cover, and cook, stirring often, until sweet potatoes are tender (paring knife can be slipped into and out of center with very little resistance), 45 minutes to 1 hour.

2. When sweet potatoes are tender, remove lid and bring sauce to rapid simmer over medium-high heat. Continue to simmer until sauce has reduced to glaze, 7 to 10 minutes.

3. for the topping Meanwhile, mix all ingredients for topping together in medium bowl; set aside.

4. Adjust oven rack to middle position and heat oven to 450 degrees. Pour sweet potato mixture into 13 by 9-inch baking dish (or shallow casserole dish of similar size). Spread topping over potatoes. Bake until pecans are toasted and crisp, 10 to 15 minutes. Serve immediately.

why this recipe works As far as vegetables go, long, verdant spears of asparagus exude elegance, and because they are forgivingly easy to cook, we are always happy to pair them with a range of sauces. For an impressive yet effortless side, we decided to top our spears in a bright, punchy vinaigrette. Broiling was our cooking method of choice because it concentrates the asparagus flavor and creates a lightly caramelized exterior. Working with thinner asparagus spears not only let us skip any tedious peeling, but they also tended to cook evenly without threat of burning. At 4 inches from the broiler, the spears achieved a perfectly charred surface without an overcooked interior. Meanwhile, we whisked together lemon juice and olive oil, flavoring the vinaigrette with shallot, fresh thyme, and Dijon for a sophisticated topping. If you want to double this recipe, use 4 pounds of asparagus and broil in 2 batches. The vinaigrettes can be doubled as well.

serves 6 to 8
total time: 15 minutes

asparagus
2 pounds thin asparagus spears, tough ends snapped off

1 tablespoon extra-virgin olive oil

Salt and pepper

lemon-shallot vinaigrette
⅓ cup extra-virgin olive oil

1 shallot, minced

1 tablespoon minced fresh thyme

1 teaspoon grated lemon zest plus 1 tablespoon juice

¼ teaspoon Dijon mustard

Salt and pepper

1. for the asparagus Adjust oven rack 4 inches from broiler element and heat broiler.

2. Toss asparagus with oil and season with salt and pepper, then lay spears in single layer on heavy rimmed baking sheet. Broil, shaking pan halfway through broiling to turn spears, until asparagus is tender and lightly browned, 8 to 10 minutes.

3. Let cool for 5 minutes and arrange on serving dish.

4. for the vinaigrette Whisk oil, shallot, thyme, lemon zest and juice, and mustard in small bowl; season to taste with salt and pepper. Drizzle vinaigrette over asparagus and serve immediately.

to make ahead
Vinaigrette can be refrigerated for up to 2 days. Let refrigerated vinaigrette sit at room temperature to allow oil to liquefy before drizzling over asparagus.

variations

asparagus with tomato-basil vinaigrette
In place of Lemon-Shallot Vinaigrette, whisk 1 cored, seeded, and minced ripe tomato, 1 minced shallot, 3 tablespoons extra-virgin olive oil, 1½ tablespoons lemon juice, and 1 tablespoon minced fresh basil in small bowl; season with salt and pepper to taste. Drizzle vinaigrette over asparagus and serve immediately.

asparagus with bacon, red onion, and balsamic vinaigrette
Fry 6 slices bacon, cut into ¼-inch pieces, in medium skillet over medium heat until crisp, about 6 minutes. Using slotted spoon, transfer bacon to paper towel–lined plate and set aside. In place of Lemon-Shallot Vinaigrette, whisk ¼ cup balsamic vinegar, ¼ cup extra-virgin olive oil, 2 tablespoons minced red onion, and 1 tablespoon minced fresh parsley in small bowl; season with salt and pepper to taste. Drizzle vinaigrette over asparagus, sprinkle with bacon, and serve immediately.

maple-glazed brussels sprouts

why this recipe works Of all the techniques we've tried, none tops braising when it comes to turning out tender, flavorful Brussels sprouts with ease. To infuse some seasonal flair into this traditional side dish, we decided to introduce maple syrup into the mix. We browned the halved sprouts in butter to establish that great caramelized flavor you'd get from roasting, and then we poured in chicken broth to begin our quick braise. Only a single tablespoon of syrup was needed to infuse the braising liquid with nuanced sweetness. To ensure the sprouts boasted complex, balanced flavor, we also stirred in minced fresh thyme and some cayenne pepper for a touch of heat. We braised the sprouts in a covered skillet, allowing the tough leaves to turn tender in minutes, and finished them off uncovered. With the braising liquid all but gone, we brought in more butter, syrup, and, for a pop of bright acidity to balance out the sweet maple taste, some cider vinegar. Choose Brussels sprouts with small, tight heads, no more than 1½ inches in diameter.

serves 8 to 10
total time: 30 minutes

4 tablespoons unsalted butter

2 pounds Brussels sprouts, trimmed and halved

½ cup chicken broth

2 tablespoons maple syrup

1 teaspoon minced fresh thyme

⅛ teaspoon cayenne pepper

4 teaspoons cider vinegar

Salt and pepper

1. Melt 2 tablespoons butter in 12-inch skillet over medium-high heat. Add Brussels sprouts and cook until browned, 6 to 8 minutes. Stir in broth, 1 tablespoon maple syrup, thyme, and cayenne and cook over medium-low heat, covered, until Brussels sprouts are nearly tender, 6 to 8 minutes.

2. Uncover and increase heat to medium-high. Cook until liquid is nearly evaporated, about 5 minutes. Off heat, stir in vinegar, remaining 2 tablespoons butter, and remaining 1 tablespoon maple syrup. Season with salt and pepper to taste, and serve.

roasted carrots with orange glaze and toasted almonds

why this recipe works Carrots have plenty of natural sweetness that comes to life when they're roasted, but cooking these vegetables to perfect tenderness can be time-consuming. We wanted to bring a side of tender, glazed carrots to the table with a minimum of prep, so we eliminated all of the peeling and slicing by using baby carrots. Creating a balanced glaze was as easy as sprinkling the carrots with brown sugar (a surefire way to boost caramelization) and a few pats of butter. Orange marmalade infused the glaze with a sweet-tart citrusy bite, and a pinch of cayenne offered welcome heat. Starting the carrots under aluminum foil allowed them to cook through as the butter and marmalade melted into a sweet, bubbling glaze. We finished the carrots off uncovered for some good browning and further caramelization. Tossing in toasted almonds and minced parsley before serving added just the crunch and freshness this simple side needed. A nonstick baking sheet will allow the carrots to get a nice roasted color and make cleanup a breeze. If you don't own one, line a traditional rimmed baking sheet with foil, but note that you may lose some of the glaze (it will seep underneath the foil) and the carrots will not brown as deeply.

serves 12
total time: 1 hour

3 pounds baby carrots

⅓ cup packed brown sugar

⅓ cup orange marmalade

4 tablespoons unsalted butter, cut into small pieces

Salt and pepper

Pinch cayenne pepper

½ cup sliced almonds, toasted

2 tablespoons minced fresh parsley

1. Adjust oven rack to lowest position and heat oven to 425 degrees.

2. Spray nonstick rimmed baking sheet with vegetable oil spray. Spread carrots over prepared baking sheet and sprinkle with sugar, marmalade, butter, ½ teaspoon salt, and cayenne. Cover tightly with aluminum foil and bake, stirring occasionally, until sugar and butter have melted and sauce is bubbling, about 25 minutes.

3. Uncover carrots and continue to cook, stirring occasionally, until tender and glazed, 20 to 30 minutes. Transfer to serving bowl, stir in almonds and parsley, season with salt and pepper to taste, and serve.

roasted cauliflower gratin

why this recipe works We created a rich but not overbearing cauliflower gratin by skipping the white sauce, instead relying on cauliflower's ability to become an ultracreamy puree to bind the dish together. We separated cauliflower heads into cores, stems, and florets, cutting the latter into slabs for even cooking. We simmered the cores, stems, and some florets in water and butter in the bottom of a Dutch oven while the remaining florets sat aloft in a steamer basket to cook off the escaping steam. Next, we blended the stem mixture into a velvety puree, thickened it with a corn-starch slurry, and stirred in the steamed florets. Topped with toasty panko and Parmesan and baked, this new take on gratin was plenty indulgent but still packed with clear cauliflower flavor. Avoid buying cauliflower with a lot of leaves, but if it cannot be avoided, buy slightly larger heads—about 2¼ pounds each.

serves 8 to 10
total time: 1 hour 30 minutes

2 heads cauliflower
(2 pounds each)

8 tablespoons unsalted butter

½ cup panko bread crumbs

2 ounces Parmesan cheese,
grated (1 cup)

Salt and pepper

½ teaspoon dry mustard

⅛ teaspoon ground nutmeg

Pinch cayenne pepper

1 teaspoon cornstarch dissolved
in 1 teaspoon water

1 tablespoon minced fresh chives

1. Adjust oven rack to middle position and heat oven to 400 degrees.

2. Pull off outer leaves of 1 head of cauliflower and trim stem. Using paring knife, cut around core to remove; halve core lengthwise and slice thin crosswise. Slice head into ½-inch-thick slabs. Cut stems from slabs to create florets that are about 1½ inches tall; slice stems thin and reserve along with sliced core. Transfer florets to bowl, including any small pieces that may have been created during trimming, and set aside. Repeat with remaining head of cauliflower (After trimming you should have about 3 cups of sliced stems and cores and 12 cups of florets.)

3. Combine sliced stems and cores, 2 cups florets, 3 cups water, and 6 tablespoons butter in Dutch oven and bring to boil over high heat. Place remaining florets in steamer basket (do not rinse bowl). Once mixture is boiling, place steamer basket in pot, cover, and reduce heat to medium. Steam florets in basket until translucent and stem ends can be easily pierced with paring knife, 10 to 12 minutes. Remove steamer basket and drain florets. Re-cover pot, reduce heat to low, and continue to cook stem mixture until very soft, about 10 minutes longer. Transfer drained florets to now-empty bowl.

4. While cauliflower is cooking, melt remaining 2 tablespoons butter in 10-inch skillet over medium heat. Add panko and cook, stirring frequently, until golden brown, 3 to 5 minutes. Transfer to bowl and let cool. Once cool, add ½ cup Parmesan and toss to combine.

5. Transfer stem mixture and cooking liquid to blender and add 2 teaspoons salt, ½ teaspoon pepper, mustard, nutmeg, cayenne, and remaining ½ cup Parmesan. Process until smooth and velvety, about 1 minute (puree should be pourable; adjust consistency with additional water as needed). With blender running, add corn-starch slurry. Season with salt and pepper to taste. Pour puree over cauliflower florets and toss gently to evenly coat. Transfer mixture to 13 by 9-inch baking dish (it will be quite loose) and smooth top with spatula.

6. Scatter bread-crumb mixture evenly over top. Transfer dish to oven and bake until sauce bubbles around edges, 13 to 15 minutes. Let stand for 20 to 25 minutes. Sprinkle with chives and serve.

to make ahead
Follow recipe through step 5, refrigerating gratin and bread crumb mixture separately for up to 24 hours. To serve, assemble and bake gratin following step 6, increasing baking time by 13 to 15 minutes.

quick green bean "casserole"

why this recipe works Green bean casserole is a holiday classic, but most recipes are fraught with overly salty canned soup and overcooked beans. To freshen up and streamline this dish, we set our sights on tender beans in a tasty sauce worthy of a prime place in our holiday spread. Rather than employing the oven and two pots—one for the beans and one for the sauce—we moved the whole production into a single skillet. Our sauce came together right around the green beans as we browned minced onion in butter, added in the beans, and amped up the flavor with fresh thyme and bay leaves. A combination of chicken broth and cream and a little flour produced a creamy, clingy, nuanced sauce. The beans steamed through right in the sauce, and finished cooking uncovered so the sauce for our not-quite casserole could thicken. Browned cremini mushrooms brought in some meaty flavor and textural contrast and as a nod to the old-school recipes that inspired this dish, we topped everything off with crunchy quick-fried shallots for a satisfying finish.

serves 8
total time: 45 minutes

3 large shallots, sliced thin (about 1 cup)

3 tablespoons all-purpose flour

Salt and pepper

5 tablespoons vegetable oil

10 ounces cremini mushrooms, trimmed and sliced ¼ inch thick

2 tablespoons unsalted butter

1 onion, chopped fine

2 garlic cloves, minced

1½ pounds green beans, trimmed

3 sprigs fresh thyme

2 bay leaves

¾ cup heavy cream

¾ cup chicken broth

1. Toss shallots with 2 tablespoons flour, ¼ teaspoon salt, and ⅛ teaspoon pepper in bowl. Heat 3 tablespoons oil in 12-inch nonstick skillet over medium-high heat until smoking; add shallots and cook, stirring frequently, until golden and crisp, about 5 minutes. Transfer shallots with oil to baking sheet lined with paper towels.

2. Wipe out skillet and return to medium-high heat. Add remaining 2 tablespoons oil, mushrooms, and ¼ teaspoon salt; cook, stirring occasionally, until mushrooms are well browned, about 8 minutes. Transfer to plate and set aside.

3. Wipe out skillet. Melt butter in skillet over medium heat, then add onion and cook, stirring occasionally, until edges begin to brown, about 2 minutes. Stir in garlic and remaining 1 tablespoon flour; toss in green beans, thyme sprigs, and bay leaves. Add cream and chicken broth, increase heat to medium-high, cover, and cook until beans are partly tender but still crisp at center, about 4 minutes. Add mushrooms and continue to cook, uncovered, until green beans are tender, about 4 minutes. Off heat, discard bay leaves and thyme sprigs; season with salt and pepper to taste. Transfer to serving dish, sprinkle evenly with shallots, and serve.

buttery sautéed peas with shallots and thyme

why this recipe works Frozen peas are blanched and flash frozen at their peak of freshness, retaining all of their natural sweetness, so it doesn't take much to turn them into a tempting accompaniment to a host of roasts. To give reliably sweet peas a touch of sophistication, we cooked them carefully and paired them with complementary (not overpowering) flavors. The subtle, mellow taste of butter-sautéed shallots promised to let the peas' flavor really shine, while thyme and garlic contributed some balanced savory flavors. Heating the peas on the broad surface of a skillet instead of a saucepan allowed them to warm through quickly and evenly, and covering the skillet sped up the cooking time further. Adding sugar to the skillet helped highlight the peas' bright, refreshing flavor. You will need a 12-inch nonstick skillet with a tight-fitting lid for this recipe.

serves 12
total time: 15 minutes

4 tablespoons unsalted butter

2 shallots, minced

1 tablespoon sugar

2 teaspoons minced fresh thyme

2 garlic cloves, minced

Salt and pepper

2 pounds frozen peas (do not thaw)

Melt butter in 12-inch nonstick skillet over medium-high heat. Add shallots, sugar, thyme, garlic, and ½ teaspoon salt and cook until softened, about 2 minutes. Stir in peas, cover, and cook until peas are heated through, 5 to 10 minutes. Season with salt and pepper to taste. Serve.

variations

buttery sautéed peas with mint and feta
Substitute 2 tablespoons minced fresh mint for thyme and sprinkle with 1½ cups crumbled feta cheese before serving.

creamy peas with tarragon
Substitute 2 tablespoons minced fresh tarragon for thyme. Before adding peas to skillet, add 1 cup heavy cream and simmer until thickened, 3 to 5 minutes.

simple cranberry sauce

why this recipe works The best cranberry sauce asserts clean, pure cranberry flavor, with enough sweetness to temper the bracingly tart fruit but not so much that the sauce is cloying or candy-like. The texture should be that of a soft gel, neither too liquidy nor too stiff, cushioning some softened but still-intact berries. In developing our own recipe, it turned out that simpler was better. We used granulated sugar as our sweetener because, unlike brown sugar, honey, or syrup, it balanced the tartness of the cranberries without introducing a distracting flavor profile of its own. Simpler was also better when it came to liquid: Like sugar, water alone kept the sauce's flavor in focus. Adding just a pinch of salt brought out an unexpected sweetness in the berries, heightening the flavor of the sauce overall. The cooking time in this recipe is intended for frozen berries. If you are using fresh cranberries, reduce the cooking time by about 2 minutes.

makes about 2½ cups
total time: 15 minutes
(plus 1 hour for cooling)

1 cup sugar

¾ cup water

12 ounces (3 cups) frozen cranberries

Salt and pepper

Bring sugar and water to boil in large saucepan over high heat, stirring occasionally to dissolve sugar. Stir in cranberries and cook over medium-low heat until slightly thickened and about two-thirds of berries have popped open, 8 to 12 minutes. Season with salt and pepper to taste. Transfer to serving bowl, cover, and let cool for at least 1 hour before serving.

variation
simple cranberry-orange sauce
Add 1 tablespoon grated orange zest with the sugar. Before cooling, stir in 2 tablespoons orange liqueur, such as triple sec or Grand Marnier.

to make ahead
Sauce can be covered and refrigerated for up to 1 week. Bring to room temperature before serving.

cranberry chutney with apples and crystallized ginger

why this recipe works There's something to be said for the simplicity of classic sweet-tart cranberry sauce, but sometimes we want more. To create a complexly flavored sauce, we looked to Indian chutneys. Adding vinegar, aromatics, and spices to slow-cooked cranberries and fruit yielded a jammy, kicked-up relish that would pair well with our favorite holiday mains. If using frozen cranberries, thaw them before cooking. Stop cooking just after the cranberries burst in step 3. The chutney will continue to thicken as it cools.

makes about 3 cups
total time: 45 minutes
(plus 1 hour for cooling)

1 teaspoon vegetable oil

1 shallot, minced

2 teaspoons grated fresh ginger

½ teaspoon salt

1 cup packed brown sugar

⅔ cup water

¼ cup cider vinegar

12 ounces (3 cups) fresh or thawed frozen cranberries

2 Granny Smith apples, peeled, cored, halved, and cut into ¼-inch pieces

⅓ cup minced crystallized ginger

1. Heat oil in medium saucepan over medium heat until shimmering. Add shallot, fresh ginger, and salt; cook, stirring occasionally, until shallot has softened, 1 to 2 minutes.

2. Add sugar, water, and vinegar. Increase heat to high and bring to simmer, stirring to dissolve sugar. Add 1½ cups cranberries and apples; return to simmer. Reduce heat to medium-low and simmer, stirring occasionally, until cranberries have almost completely broken down and mixture has thickened, about 15 minutes.

3. Add crystallized ginger and remaining 1½ cups cranberries; continue to simmer, stirring occasionally, until cranberries just begin to burst, 5 to 7 minutes. Transfer to bowl and let cool for at least 1 hour before serving.

variations

cranberry chutney with fennel and golden raisins
Increase oil to 2 teaspoons and substitute 1 cored fennel bulb cut into ¼-inch pieces and ½ teaspoon fennel seeds for fresh ginger. Increase cooking time in step 1 to 5 minutes. Increase water to 1 cup, omit apples, and substitute golden raisins for crystallized ginger.

cranberry chutney with pear, lemon, and rosemary
Remove two 2-inch strips zest from 1 lemon, then cut away peel and pith. Holding fruit over bowl, use paring knife to slice between membranes to release segments. Set aside zest and segments. Substitute chopped fresh rosemary for fresh ginger. Substitute 2 Bosc pears, peeled and cut into ¼-inch pieces, for apples and omit crystallized ginger. Add lemon zest and segments to pot with cranberries in step 2.

cranberry-orange chutney
Remove four 2-inch strips zest from 1 orange, then cut away peel and pith from orange plus 1 additional orange. Holding fruit over bowl, use paring knife to slice between membranes to release segments. Set aside zest and segments. Increase fresh ginger to 4 teaspoons and add 1 teaspoon yellow mustard seeds to oil with fresh ginger in step 1. Increase water to ¾ cup and add orange zest and segments to pot with cranberries in step 2. Omit apples and crystallized ginger.

spicy cranberry chutney
Increase oil to 2 teaspoons and substitute 1 stemmed and seeded red bell pepper, cut into ¼-inch pieces, and 2 stemmed, seeded, and minced jalapeños for fresh ginger in step 1. Increase cooking time in step 1 to 5 minutes. Increase water to ¾ cup and omit apples and crystallized ginger.

to make ahead
Chutney can be refrigerated for up to 3 days. Bring to room temperature before serving.

basic bread stuffing

why this recipe works Hearty, rustic, and supersavory, bread stuffing is a staple in any holiday spread. Our recipe streamlines this classic, using cubed bread, sautéed onions and celery, and a smattering of spices. After toasting plenty of bread cubes, we browned a goodly portion of butter to unlock its rich, nutty flavor and used much of it to impart some deep browning to chopped onions and celery. Poultry seasoning, bloomed among the vegetables, offered balanced, savory taste. Chicken broth promised a meaty character similar to that achieved by baking stuffing inside of a turkey, so we reduced it on the stovetop and stirred more into the bread and vegetables to moisten the stuffing and tie its flavors together. Browned butter drizzled on before baking created a toasty crust. Use hearty white sandwich bread here; other types of bread will yield a chewy, less moist stuffing.

serves 10 to 12
total time: 2 hours

2 pounds hearty white sandwich bread, cut into ½-inch cubes (16 cups)

16 tablespoons (2 sticks) unsalted butter, cut into 16 pieces

4 onions, chopped fine

4 celery ribs, minced

4 teaspoons poultry seasoning

1¾ teaspoons salt

1 teaspoon pepper

6 cups chicken broth

1. Adjust oven racks to upper-middle and lower-middle positions and heat oven to 325 degrees. Divide bread between 2 rimmed baking sheets and bake until golden brown, 50 to 55 minutes, stirring bread and switching and rotating sheets halfway through baking. Let cool completely on sheets, then transfer to large bowl.

2. Melt butter in 12-inch skillet over medium-low heat. Cook, stirring constantly, until butter is nutty brown, 5 to 7 minutes. Reserve 3 tablespoons browned butter in small bowl. Add onions and celery to skillet, increase heat to medium, and cook until browned, 12 to 15 minutes. Stir in poultry seasoning, salt, and pepper and cook until fragrant, about 30 seconds. Add vegetable mixture to bowl with toasted bread.

3. Increase oven temperature to 425 degrees. Add 2 cups broth to now-empty skillet and cook over high heat, scraping up any browned bits, until reduced to 1 cup, 6 to 8 minutes. Combine remaining 4 cups broth and reduced broth with vegetable-bread mixture and let sit for 10 minutes, stirring once. Transfer stuffing to 13 by 9-inch baking dish and press into even layer. Drizzle reserved browned butter evenly over top and bake on upper rack until golden brown and crisp, 35 to 45 minutes. Let cool for 15 minutes. Serve.

to make ahead
Stuffing without butter topping can be refrigerated in baking dish, covered with aluminum foil, for up to 24 hours. To finish, remove foil, drizzle with melted reserved browned butter, re-cover, and bake for 10 minutes at 425 degrees. Uncover and bake until stuffing is heated through and top is golden brown, 35 to 40 minutes.

homemade cornbread dressing

why this recipe works Some things are best made from scratch, and for our cornbread dressing, we didn't want to cut any corners. Since the dressing's mix-ins would introduce lots of flavors and textures, we prepared a simple cornbread and then cubed the cooled bread and toasted it (which worked just as well as staling the bread overnight). This savory cornbread was primed to compete with plenty of big flavors, so we loaded the dressing with pork sausage, herbs, and aromatics. A custardy mixture of half-and-half and eggs (plus a pinch of cayenne for some heat) bound it together, and a drizzle of butter added before baking made for a rich finish. Use fine or coarse cornmeal.

serves 10 to 12
total time: 3 hours
(plus 2 hours 45 minutes
for cooling)

cornbread
2⅔ cups milk

½ cup vegetable oil

4 large eggs

2 cups cornmeal

2 cups all-purpose flour

4 teaspoons baking powder

1 teaspoon salt

dressing
1½ pounds bulk pork sausage

2 onions, chopped fine

3 celery ribs, chopped fine

6 tablespoons unsalted butter

4 garlic cloves, minced

1 teaspoon dried sage

1 teaspoon dried thyme

3½ cups chicken broth

1 cup half-and-half

4 large eggs

½ teaspoon salt

⅛ teaspoon cayenne pepper

1. for the cornbread Adjust oven racks to upper-middle and lower-middle positions and heat oven to 375 degrees. Grease and flour 13- by 9-inch baking pan. Whisk milk, oil, and eggs in bowl; set aside. Combine cornmeal, flour, baking powder, and salt in large bowl. Add milk mixture, whisking until smooth. Pour batter into prepared pan and bake on lower rack until golden and toothpick inserted in center comes out clean, about 30 minutes. Let cool in pan on wire rack, about 2 hours.

2. Heat oven to 250 degrees. Cut cornbread into 1-inch squares. Divide cornbread between 2 rimmed baking sheets and bake until dry, 50 minutes to 1 hour, switching and rotating sheets halfway through baking. Let cornbread cool completely on sheets, about 30 minutes.

3. for the dressing Cook sausage in 12-inch nonstick skillet over medium-high heat until no longer pink, about 5 minutes. Transfer sausage to paper towel-lined plate and pour off all but 2 tablespoons fat from pan. Add onions, celery,

and 2 tablespoons butter to fat in pan and cook until softened, about 5 minutes. Add garlic, sage, and thyme and cook until fragrant about 30 seconds. Stir in broth, remove from heat, and let cool for 5 minutes.

4. Whisk half-and-half, eggs, salt, and cayenne in large bowl. Slowly whisk in warm broth mixture until incorporated. Fold in dried cornbread and reserved sausage and let sit, tossing occasionally, until saturated, about 20 minutes.

5. Heat oven to 375 degrees. Grease 13- by 9-inch baking pan. Transfer soaked cornbread to prepared pan. Melt remaining butter and drizzle evenly over top. Bake on upper rack until surface is golden brown and crisp, 30 to 40 minutes. Let cool for 15 minutes. Serve.

to make ahead
Cornbread can be baked and left in its pan up to 2 days in advance. Instead of oven-drying in step 2, stale cubed cornbread overnight at room temperature.

wild rice dressing

why this recipe works Combining hearty bread stuffing with earthy wild rice, this rich, rustic dressing is just the change of pace we always welcome on our holiday table. Different varieties of wild rice absorb varying amounts of liquid, so we boiled ours in water and chicken broth before draining and reserving the cooking liquid. Pea-size bread crumbs kept the bread from overshadowing the rice, and baking them briefly added color and crunch. We sautéed onions and celery in butter and added garlic, sage, and thyme for a savory boost. A blend of eggs and cream enriched and bound the dressing together while some of the starchy cooking liquid enhanced the nutty flavor of the rice. If you have less than 1½ cups of leftover rice cooking liquid, make up the difference with additional chicken broth.

serves 10 to 12
total time: 3 hours

2 cups chicken broth

2 cups water

1 bay leaf

2 cups wild rice

10 slices hearty white sandwich bread, torn into pieces

8 tablespoons unsalted butter

2 onions, chopped fine

3 celery ribs, minced

4 garlic cloves, minced

1½ teaspoons dried sage

1½ teaspoons dried thyme

1½ cups heavy cream

2 large eggs

¾ teaspoon salt

½ teaspoon pepper

1. Bring broth, water, and bay leaf to boil in medium saucepan over medium-high heat. Add rice, reduce heat to low, and simmer, covered, until rice is tender, 35 to 45 minutes. Strain contents of pan through fine-mesh strainer into 4-cup liquid measuring cup. Transfer rice to bowl; discard bay leaf. Measure out 1½ cups cooking liquid and set aside.

2. Adjust oven racks to upper-middle and lower-middle positions and heat oven to 325 degrees. Pulse half of bread in food processor into pea-size pieces, about 6 pulses; transfer to rimmed baking sheet. Repeat with remaining bread and second rimmed baking sheet. Bake bread crumbs until golden, about 20 minutes, stirring occasionally and switching and rotating sheets halfway through baking. Let cool completely, about 10 minutes.

3. Melt 4 tablespoons butter in 12-inch skillet over medium heat. Cook onions and celery until softened and golden, 8 to 10 minutes. Add garlic, sage, and thyme and cook until fragrant, about 30 seconds. Stir in reserved cooking liquid, remove from heat, and let cool for 5 minutes.

4. Whisk cream, eggs, salt, and pepper together in large bowl. Slowly whisk in warm broth-vegetable mixture. Stir in rice and toasted bread crumbs and transfer to 13 by 9-inch baking dish.

5. Melt remaining 4 tablespoons butter in now-empty skillet and drizzle evenly over dressing. Cover dish with aluminum foil and bake on lower rack until set, 45 to 55 minutes. Remove foil and let cool for 15 minutes. Serve.

variations
dried fruit and nut wild rice dressing
Add 1½ cups chopped dried apricots, cranberries, or cherries and 1½ cups chopped toasted pecans with bread crumbs in step 4.

leek and mushroom wild rice dressing
Substitute 4 leeks (white and light green parts only), halved lengthwise and sliced thin, and 10 ounces cremini mushrooms, sliced thin, for onions and celery.

to make ahead
Assembled dressing can be refrigerated in baking dish, covered with aluminum foil, for up to 24 hours following step 4. Increase baking time to 1 hour 5 minutes to 1¼ hours.

creamy corn pudding

why this recipe works Sweet, savory, and supremely creamy, corn pudding is a Thanksgiving mainstay. When we created this recipe we wanted to offer smooth custard (one that didn't curdle or weep) loaded with fresh corn taste. A combination of whole and grated kernels, as well as the "milk" from the cobs (which we collected by scraping the cleaned cobs with the back of a butter knife) delivered big corn flavor and an appealing texture. Sautéing the corn in butter before simmering it in heavy cream eliminated much of the corn's own liquid, banned any unsightly weeping, and deepened the sweet corn flavor. Cooking the pudding in a water bath prevented curdling for an even, creamy texture, and cayenne added some heat to counter the corn's natural sweetness. This recipe should be served hot and cannot be reheated, so plan ahead accordingly.

serves 6
total time: 1 hour 15 minutes

6 ears corn, husks and silk removed

3 tablespoons unsalted butter, plus extra for baking dish

⅔ cup heavy cream

1½ teaspoons salt

1 teaspoon sugar

¼ teaspoon cayenne pepper

1⅓ cups whole milk

4 large eggs, lightly beaten

1 tablespoon cornstarch

1. Cut kernels from 5 ears corn into medium bowl, then scrape cobs with back of butter knife over bowl to collect milk (you should have about 2½ cups kernels and milk). Grate remaining 1 ear corn on coarse side of box grater (you should have about ½ cup grated kernels). Add grated kernels to bowl with cut kernels.

2. Adjust oven rack to lower-middle position, place roasting pan or large baking dish on rack, and heat oven to 350 degrees. Generously butter 8-inch square baking dish. Bring 2 quarts water to boil in kettle or saucepan.

3. Melt butter in 12-inch skillet over medium heat. Add corn and cook, stirring occasionally, until corn is bright yellow and liquid has almost evaporated, about 5 minutes. Add cream, salt, sugar, and cayenne and cook, stirring occasionally, until thickened and spoon leaves trail when pan bottom is scraped, about 5 minutes. Transfer mixture to medium bowl. Stir milk into mixture, then whisk in eggs and cornstarch. Pour mixture into buttered baking dish.

4. Set filled dish in roasting pan or large baking dish already in oven. Fill outer pan with boiling water to reach halfway up inner dish. Bake until center jiggles slightly when shaken and pudding has browned lightly in spots, 20 to 25 minutes. Remove baking dish from water bath, let cool for 10 minutes, and serve.

lentil salad with pomegranate and walnuts

why this recipe works A simple lentil salad is a great way to bring bright, fresh flavor to holiday spreads often dominated by rich, creamy sides. For lentils with a perfectly firm-tender bite, we began by brining them in warm salt water, which softened their skins to prevent blowouts. For further insurance, we cooked the lentils in the oven, where the gentle indirect heat turned them uniformly tender. To transform these earthy legumes into an impressive, seasonal side, all we had left to do was to pair them with a tart vinaigrette, pomegranate seeds for juicy pops of sweetness, and some crunchy walnuts. French green lentils, or lentilles du Puy, are our preferred choice for this recipe, but it works with any type of lentil except red or yellow. Brining helps keep the lentils intact but they'll still taste good without it. The salad can be served warm or at room temperature.

serves 4 to 6
total time: 1 hour
(plus 1 hour for soaking)

1 cup lentils, picked over and rinsed

Salt and pepper

2 cups chicken broth

5 garlic cloves, lightly crushed and peeled

1 bay leaf

5 tablespoons extra-virgin olive oil

3 tablespoons lemon juice

1 shallot, minced

¼ cup chopped fresh cilantro

⅓ cup walnuts, toasted and chopped coarse

⅓ cup pomegranate seeds

1. Place lentils and 1 teaspoon salt in bowl. Cover with 4 cups warm water (about 110 degrees) and soak for 1 hour. Drain well.

2. Adjust oven rack to middle position and heat oven to 325 degrees. Place drained lentils, 2 cups water, broth, garlic, bay leaf, and ½ teaspoon salt in medium saucepan. Cover and bake until lentils are tender but remain intact, 40 minutes to 1 hour. Meanwhile, whisk oil and lemon juice together in large bowl.

3. Drain lentils well; remove and discard garlic and bay leaf. Add drained lentils, shallot, cilantro, half of walnuts, and half of pomegranate seeds to dressing and toss to combine. Season with salt and pepper to taste. Transfer to serving dish, sprinkle with remaining walnuts and pomegranate seeds, and serve.

variations

lentil salad with olives, mint, and feta
Substitute white wine vinegar for lemon juice. Omit walnuts and pomegranate seeds and add ½ cup coarsely chopped pitted kalamata olives and ½ cup minced fresh mint with lentils and shallot in step 3. Sprinkle with 1 ounce crumbled feta before serving.

lentil salad with hazelnuts and goat cheese
Substitute red wine vinegar for lemon juice and add 2 teaspoons Dijon mustard to dressing in step 2. Omit walnuts and pomegranate seeds and substitute chopped parsley for cilantro. Sprinkle with 2 ounces crumbled goat cheese and ⅓ cup coarsely chopped toasted hazelnuts before serving.

lentil salad with carrots and cilantro
Toss 2 carrots, peeled and cut into 2-inch-long matchsticks, with 1 teaspoon ground cumin, ½ teaspoon ground cinnamon, and ⅛ teaspoon cayenne pepper in bowl. Cover and microwave until carrots are tender but still crisp, 2 to 4 minutes. Omit shallot, walnuts, and pomegranate seeds. Add carrots with lentils and cilantro in step 3.

to make ahead
Drained brined lentils can be refrigerated for up to 2 days before cooking.

wild rice pilaf with pecans and cranberries

why this recipe works Properly cooked wild rice is chewy yet tender, and pleasingly rustic—not disappointingly crunchy or gluey. We wanted to turn out fluffy pilaf-style grains loaded with festive mix-ins. After a few trials, we found that simmering the rice in plenty of liquid and then draining it was the most reliable cooking method. A combination of water and chicken broth infused with thyme and bay leaves produced rice with nuanced savory flavor. We prepared a batch of white rice (boosted with sautéed chopped onion and carrot and studded with plumped dried cranberries) to stir in with the wild rice as a means of balancing out the latter's earthy qualities. For even more variation in this otherwise simple side, we stirred in nutty toasted pecans and minced parsley for instant freshness.

serves 6 to 8
total time: 1 hour 15 minutes

1¾ cups chicken broth

2½ cups water

2 bay leaves

8 sprigs fresh thyme, divided into 2 bundles, each tied together with kitchen twine

1 cup wild rice, picked over and rinsed

3 tablespoons unsalted butter

1 onion, chopped fine

1 large carrot, peeled and chopped fine

Salt and pepper

1½ cups long-grain white rice, rinsed

¾ cup dried cranberries

¾ cup pecans, toasted and chopped coarse

1½ tablespoons minced fresh parsley

1. Bring broth, ¼ cup water, bay leaves, and 1 bundle thyme to boil in medium saucepan over medium-high heat. Add wild rice, cover, and reduce heat to low; simmer until rice is plump and tender and has absorbed most of liquid, 35 to 45 minutes. Drain rice in fine-mesh strainer to remove excess liquid. Remove bay leaves and thyme. Return rice to now-empty saucepan, cover, and set aside.

2. Meanwhile, melt butter in medium saucepan over medium-high heat. Add onion, carrot, and 1 teaspoon salt and cook, stirring frequently, until vegetables are softened but not browned, about 4 minutes. Add white rice and stir to coat grains with butter; cook, stirring frequently, until grains begin to turn translucent, about 3 minutes. Meanwhile, bring remaining 2¼ cups water to boil in small saucepan or in microwave. Add boiling water and second thyme bundle to rice and return to boil. Reduce heat to low, sprinkle cranberries evenly over rice, and cover. Simmer until all liquid is absorbed, 16 to 18 minutes. Off heat, remove thyme and fluff rice with fork.

3. Combine wild rice, white rice mixture, pecans, and parsley in large bowl and toss with rubber spatula. Season with salt and pepper to taste; serve immediately.

variation

wild rice pilaf with scallions, cilantro, and almonds
Omit dried cranberries. Substitute ¾ cup toasted sliced almonds for pecans and 2 tablespoons minced fresh cilantro for parsley. Add 2 thinly sliced scallions and 1 teaspoon lime juice with almonds.

to make ahead
Following step 2, wild rice and white rice mixture can be combined in large bowl and refrigerated for up to 3 days. To serve, cover bowl and microwave until hot, 3 to 5 minutes, fluffing with fork halfway through microwaving. Proceed with step 3 with addition of pecans and parsley.

brown rice salad with asparagus, goat cheese, and lemon

why this recipe works This fresh, hearty side dish will stand out among its richer, creamier counterparts on the holiday table. We achieved perfectly cooked brown rice by boiling it in abundant water. Sprinkling the rice with bright lemon juice while it was still warm boosted its flavor. To easily turn our brown rice into an appealing side salad, we stirred in crisp, browned bites of asparagus, more lemon juice, creamy goat cheese, and crunchy toasted almonds. We like the flavor of brown basmati rice, but any long-grain brown rice is acceptable. Look for asparagus that is bright green and firm. Toast the almonds in a skillet (without any oil) set over medium heat, shaking the pan occasionally to prevent scorching.

serves 6 to 8
total time: 1 hour 15 minutes

brown rice
1½ cups long-grain brown rice

2 teaspoons salt

2 teaspoons lemon juice

asparagus and vinaigrette
1 tablespoon vegetable oil

1 pound asparagus, trimmed

Salt and pepper

2½ tablespoons extra-virgin olive oil

1 shallot, minced

1 teaspoon grated lemon zest plus 2 tablespoons juice

4 ounces goat cheese, crumbled (1 cup)

½ cup slivered almonds, toasted

¼ cup chopped fresh parsley

1. for the brown rice Bring 3 quarts water to boil in large pot. Add rice and salt; cook, stirring occasionally, until rice is tender, 22 to 25 minutes. Drain rice, transfer to parchment paper–lined rimmed baking sheet, and spread into even layer. Drizzle rice with lemon juice and let cool completely, about 15 minutes.

2. for the asparagus and vinaigrette Heat vegetable oil in 12-inch skillet over medium-high heat until shimmering. Add half of asparagus with tips pointed in 1 direction and remaining asparagus with tips pointed in opposite direction. Using tongs, arrange spears in even layer (they will not quite fit into single layer); cover and cook until bright green and still crisp, 2 to 5 minutes. Uncover, increase heat to high, season with salt and pepper, and continue to cook until tender and well browned on 1 side, 5 to 7 minutes, using tongs to occasionally move spears from center to edge of pan to ensure all are browned. Transfer to plate and let cool completely. Cut into 1-inch pieces.

3. Whisk olive oil, shallot, lemon zest and juice, ½ teaspoon salt, and ½ teaspoon pepper together in bowl. Transfer cooled rice to large bowl. Add asparagus, all but 2 tablespoons goat cheese, and dressing; toss to combine. Let stand for 10 minutes.

4. Add ⅓ cup almonds and 3 tablespoons parsley; toss to combine. Season with salt and pepper to taste. Sprinkle with remaining almonds, reserved 2 tablespoons goat cheese, and remaining 1 tablespoon parsley; serve.

ultimate flaky buttermilk biscuits

why this recipe works For our biscuits to qualify as the be-all and end-all, they needed to have innumerable, ethereally thin layers, and they needed to be baked with a minimum of fuss. First, for an even distribution of butter (and all of the small air pockets that it produces), we froze whole sticks and grated all but 1 tablespoon from each into a mixture of flour, sugar, baking powder, baking soda, and salt. High-protein King Arthur flour promised more gluten and therefore a more structured, stable crumb. Buttermilk gave the biscuits pleasant tang, which we balanced out with sugar. For maximum layers, we rolled and folded the dough a total of five times, turning the dough from shaggy to smooth, and we bypassed the biscuit cutter in favor of square biscuits. Letting the dough rest for 30 minutes and trimming away the creased edges ensured that these biscuits rose up nice and tall in the oven. A brush of melted butter reinforced the biscuits' flavor and ensured a lovely golden brown hue. We prefer King Arthur all-purpose flour for this recipe, but other brands will work. Use sticks of butter. In hot or humid environments, chill the flour mixture, grater, and work bowls before use. The dough will start out crumbly and dry in pockets but will be smooth by the end of the folding process; do not add extra buttermilk. Flour the counter and the top of the dough as needed to prevent sticking, but be careful not to incorporate large pockets of flour into the dough while folding.

makes 9 biscuits
total time: 2 hours

3 cups (15 ounces) King Arthur all-purpose flour

2 tablespoons sugar

4 teaspoons baking powder

½ teaspoon baking soda

1½ teaspoons salt

16 tablespoons (2 sticks) unsalted butter, frozen for 30 minutes

1¼ cups buttermilk, chilled

1. Line rimmed baking sheet with parchment paper and set aside. Whisk flour, sugar, baking powder, baking soda, and salt together in large bowl. Coat sticks of butter in flour mixture, then grate 7 tablespoons from each stick on large holes of box grater directly into flour mixture. Toss gently to combine. Set aside remaining 2 tablespoons butter.

2. Add buttermilk to flour mixture and fold with spatula until just combined (dough will look dry). Transfer dough to liberally floured counter. Dust surface of dough with flour; using your floured hands, press dough into rough 7-inch square.

3. Roll dough into 12 by 9-inch rectangle with short side parallel to edge of counter. Starting at bottom of dough, fold into thirds like business letter, using bench scraper or metal spatula to release dough from counter. Press top of dough firmly to seal folds. Turn dough 90 degrees clockwise. Repeat rolling into 12 by 9-inch rectangle, folding into thirds, and turning clockwise 4 more times, for total of 5 sets of folds. After last set of folds, roll dough into 8½-inch square about 1 inch thick. Transfer dough to prepared sheet, cover with plastic wrap, and refrigerate for 30 minutes. Adjust oven rack to upper-middle position and heat oven to 400 degrees.

4. Transfer dough to lightly floured cutting board. Using sharp, floured chef's knife, trim ¼ inch of dough from each side of square and discard. Cut remaining dough into 9 squares, flouring knife after each cut. Arrange biscuits at least 1 inch apart on sheet. Melt reserved butter; brush tops of biscuits with melted butter.

5. Bake until tops are golden brown, 22 to 25 minutes, rotating sheet halfway through baking. Transfer biscuits to wire rack and let cool for 15 minutes before serving.

to make ahead
Biscuits are best served immediately after baking, but if you wish to bake a day ahead, warm them before serving, reheating for 10 to 15 minutes in 300-degree oven.

fluffy dinner rolls

why this recipe works Dinner rolls are great freshly baked, but they quickly lose those qualities as they cool. For rolls we could bake in advance, we applied a Japanese bread-making technique that boosts dough's moisture by using a flour paste. We prepared the paste by heating and whisking flour and water to a pudding-like texture and then gradually incorporated the milk, an egg, flour, and yeast one after the other. We let the dough rest to encourage strong gluten formation before adding salt, sugar, and butter. Flattening portions of dough and rolling them into spirals created complex coiled layers, which baked up into feathery sheets. These rolls were incredibly light, and, best of all, they were just as good when reheated a day later. We strongly recommend weighing the flour for the dough. The tackiness of the dough aids in flattening and stretching it in step 5, so do not flour your counter. This recipe requires letting the dough rest for at least 2 hours before baking.

makes 12 rolls
total time: 1 hour 45 minutes
(plus 1 hour 45 minutes for rising)

flour paste
½ cup water

3 tablespoons bread flour

dough
½ cup cold milk

1 large egg

2 cups (11 ounces) bread flour

1½ teaspoons instant or rapid-rise yeast

2 tablespoons sugar

1 teaspoon salt

4 tablespoons unsalted butter, softened, plus ½ tablespoon, melted

1. for the flour paste Whisk water and flour together in small bowl until no lumps remain. Microwave, whisking every 20 seconds, until mixture thickens to stiff, smooth, pudding-like consistency that forms mound when dropped from end of whisk into bowl, 40 to 80 seconds.

2. for the dough In bowl of stand mixer, whisk flour paste and milk together until smooth. Add egg and whisk until incorporated. Add flour and yeast. Fit stand mixer with dough hook and mix on low speed until all flour is moistened, 1 to 2 minutes. Let stand for 15 minutes.

3. Add sugar and salt and mix on medium-low speed for 5 minutes. With mixer running, add softened butter, 1 tablespoon at a time. Continue to mix on medium-low speed 5 minutes longer, scraping down dough hook and sides of bowl occasionally (dough will stick to bottom of bowl).

4. Transfer dough to very lightly floured counter. Knead briefly to form ball and transfer, seam side down, to lightly greased bowl; lightly coat surface of dough with vegetable oil spray and cover with plastic wrap. Let rise until doubled in volume, about 1 hour.

5. Grease 9-inch round cake pan and set aside. Transfer dough to counter. Press dough gently but firmly to expel all air. Pat and stretch dough to form 8 by 9-inch rectangle with short side facing you. Cut dough lengthwise into 4 equal strips and cut each strip crosswise into 3 equal pieces. Working with 1 piece at a time, stretch and press dough gently to form 8 by 2-inch strip. Starting on short side, roll dough to form snug cylinder and arrange shaped rolls seam side down in prepared pan, placing 10 rolls around edge of pan, pointing inward, and remaining 2 rolls in center. Cover with plastic and let rise until doubled, 45 minutes to 1 hour.

6. When rolls are nearly doubled, adjust oven rack to lowest position and heat oven to 375 degrees. Bake rolls until deep golden brown, 25 to 30 minutes. Let rolls cool in pan on wire rack for 3 minutes; invert rolls onto rack, then re-invert. Brush tops and sides of rolls with melted butter. Let rolls cool for at least 20 minutes before serving.

to make ahead
Rolls can be made a day ahead. To refresh them before serving, wrap them in aluminum foil and heat them in a 350-degree oven for 15 minutes.

sweet
endings

chocolate truffles

why this recipe works Truffles are the ultimate indulgence, and ours are creamy and silky-smooth thanks to a few key tricks. First, we stirred warm cream into melted chocolate for a smooth consistency; using corn syrup rather than sugar secured the perfect texture and butter gave us a supersilky ganache. Gradually cooling the ganache before rolling the truffles staved off grainy sugar crystals, and rolling each truffle in confectioners' sugar and cocoa powder gave our simple treats a professional finish. In step 5, running your knife under hot water and wiping it dry makes cutting the chocolate easier. We prefer truffles made with 60 percent bittersweet chocolate. Our favorite brands are Ghirardelli and Callebaut.

makes 64 truffles
total time: 45 minutes
(plus 6 hours for
cooling and chilling)

ganache
12 ounces bittersweet chocolate, chopped coarse

½ cup heavy cream

2 tablespoons light corn syrup

½ teaspoon vanilla extract

Pinch salt

1½ tablespoons unsalted butter, cut into 8 pieces and softened

coating
1 cup (3 ounces) Dutch-processed cocoa

¼ cup (1 ounce) confectioners' sugar

1. for the ganache Lightly coat 8-inch baking pan with vegetable oil spray. Make parchment sling by folding 2 long sheets of parchment so that they are as wide as baking pan. Lay sheets of parchment in pan perpendicular to each other, with extra hanging over edges of pan. Push parchment into corners and up sides of pan, smoothing flush to pan.

2. Microwave chocolate in medium bowl at 50 percent power, stirring occasionally, until mostly melted and few small chocolate pieces remain, 2 to 3 minutes; set aside. Microwave cream in measuring cup until warm to touch, about 30 seconds. Stir corn syrup, vanilla, and salt into cream and pour mixture over chocolate. Cover bowl with plastic wrap, set aside for 3 minutes, and then stir with wooden spoon to combine. Stir in butter, 1 piece at a time, until fully incorporated.

3. Using rubber spatula, transfer ganache to prepared pan and set aside at room temperature for 2 hours. Cover pan and transfer to refrigerator; chill for at least 2 hours.

4. for the coating Sift cocoa and sugar through fine-mesh strainer into large bowl. Sift again into large cake pan and set aside.

5. Gripping overhanging parchment, lift ganache from pan. Cut ganache into sixty-four 1-inch squares (8 rows by 8 rows). (If ganache cracks during slicing, let sit at room temperature for 5 to 10 minutes and then proceed.) Dust your hands lightly with cocoa mixture to prevent ganache from sticking and roll each square into ball. Transfer balls to cake pan with cocoa mixture and roll to evenly coat. Lightly shake truffles in your hand over pan to remove excess coating. Repeat until all ganache squares are rolled and coated. Cover and refrigerate for at least 2 hours. Let truffles sit at room temperature for 5 to 10 minutes before serving.

variations
hazelnut-mocha truffles
Substitute 2 tablespoons Frangelico (hazelnut-flavored liqueur) and 1 tablespoon espresso powder for vanilla. For coating, omit confectioners' sugar and use enough cocoa to coat your hands while shaping truffles. Roll shaped truffles in 1½ cups finely chopped toasted hazelnuts.

chocolate chai masala truffles
Increase heavy cream to ½ cup plus 3 tablespoons. After microwaving in step 2, steep 2 chai tea bags in cream for 5 minutes, remove tea bags, and microwave until warm again, about 20 seconds, before proceeding with recipe. For coating, sift 1 teaspoon ground cinnamon with cocoa and confectioners' sugar.

to make ahead
Ganache can be stored, refrigerated, for up to 2 days. Finished truffles can be stored, refrigerated, for up to 1 week.

glazed butter cookies

why this recipe works Rich, sweet glazed butter cookies are a holiday mainstay, and to make them reliably crisp with a fine, even crumb, we made some important substitutions. Superfine sugar brought sweetness without the overly flaky texture granulated sugar can create. Without leaveners or eggs in the dough, we were guaranteed moist, chewy cookies void of air pockets. Using the reverse-creaming method—beating butter into flour and sugar—further prevented air bubbles for cookies that baked up flat, sturdy, and crisp—perfect for glazing and decorating. Beating in soft, tangy cream cheese made the dough particularly easy to work with while adding nice flavor. Cold, firm dough stamps out more cleanly than soft, so we chilled it after rolling. Cut shapes close together, starting from the edges and working your way to the middle to use as much dough as possible and reduce scraps. Overworked dough leads to tough cookies. Make sure to chill dough scraps again before rolling them out a second time. Cookies can be finished with sprinkles or other decorations immediately after glazing.

makes about 38 cookies
total time: 1 hour
(plus 1 hour 15 minutes
for chilling and cooling)

cookies
2½ cups (12½ ounces) all-purpose flour

¾ cup (5¼ ounces) superfine sugar

¼ teaspoon salt

16 tablespoons (2 sticks) unsalted butter, cut into 16 pieces and softened

2 tablespoons cream cheese, room temperature

2 teaspoons vanilla extract

glaze
1 tablespoon cream cheese, room temperature

3 tablespoons milk

1½ cups (6 ounces) confectioners' sugar

1. for the cookies Using stand mixer fitted with paddle, mix flour, sugar, and salt at low speed until combined, about 5 seconds. With mixer running on low, add butter 1 piece at a time; continue to mix until mixture looks crumbly and slightly wet, 1 to 2 minutes longer. Beat in cream cheese and vanilla until dough just begins to form large clumps, about 30 seconds.

2. Knead dough by hand in bowl, 2 or 3 turns, until it forms large, cohesive mass. Transfer dough to counter and divide it into 2 even pieces. Press each piece into 4-inch disk, wrap disks in plastic wrap, and refrigerate until dough is firm but malleable, about 30 minutes.

3. Adjust oven rack to middle position and heat oven to 375 degrees. Line 2 rimmed baking sheets with parchment paper. Working with 1 piece of dough at a time, roll ⅛ inch thick between 2 large sheets of parchment paper; slide rolled dough, still on parchment, onto baking sheets and refrigerate until firm, about 10 minutes.

4. Working with 1 sheet of dough at a time, peel parchment from 1 side of dough and cut into desired shapes using cookie cutters; space cookies 1½ inches apart on prepared sheets. Bake 1 sheet at a time until cookies are light golden brown, about 10 minutes, rotating sheet halfway through baking. (Dough scraps can be patted together, chilled, and rerolled once.) Let cookies cool on sheet for 3 minutes; transfer cookies to wire rack and let cool to room temperature.

5. for the glaze Whisk cream cheese and 2 tablespoons milk in medium bowl until combined and no lumps remain. Add sugar and whisk until smooth, adding remaining 1 tablespoon milk as needed until glaze is thin enough to spread easily. Using back of spoon, drizzle or spread scant teaspoon of glaze onto each cooled cookie. Allow glazed cookies to dry at least 30 minutes before serving.

to make ahead
Wrapped dough can be refrigerated for up to 3 days or frozen up to 2 weeks; defrost in refrigerator before rolling.

soft and chewy gingerbread cookies

why this recipe works The comforting aroma of gingerbread cookies is the harbinger of the holiday season, and to include these chewy, fragrant treats on our cookie tray, we needed a spiced, easy-to-roll dough. Incorporating plenty of melted butter into the dry ingredients with a food processor created a firm but workable dough. Cinnamon, ginger, and cloves offered classic gingerbread flavor, and brown sugar reinforced the molasses we added in with the butter. Rolling the chilled dough to a ¼-inch thickness produced soft, chewy cookies every time. No gingerbread cookies should go unadorned, so we whipped egg whites and sugar for a structured, easy-to-apply frosting that boasted a bright white gloss. Let the melted butter cool before adding it in step 1, or the dough will be too sticky to work with. We roll the dough between sheets of parchment paper (with no additional flour), so scraps can be rerolled as many times as necessary.

makes about 24 cookies
total time: 1 hour
(plus 1 hour for chilling)

3 cups (15 ounces) all-purpose flour

¾ cup packed (5¼ ounces) dark brown sugar

1 tablespoon ground cinnamon

1 tablespoon ground ginger

¾ teaspoon baking soda

½ teaspoon ground cloves

½ teaspoon salt

12 tablespoons unsalted butter, melted and cooled

¾ cup molasses

2 tablespoons milk

1. Process flour, sugar, cinnamon, ginger, baking soda, cloves, and salt in food processor until combined, about 10 seconds. Add melted butter, molasses, and milk and process until soft dough forms and no streaks of flour remain, about 20 seconds, scraping down sides of bowl as needed.

2. Spray counter lightly with baking spray with flour, transfer dough to counter, and knead until dough forms cohesive ball, about 20 seconds. Divide dough in half. Form each half into 5-inch disk, wrap disks tightly in plastic wrap, and refrigerate for at least 1 hour.

3. Adjust oven racks to upper-middle and lower-middle positions and heat oven to 350 degrees. Line 2 rimmed baking sheets with parchment paper. Working with 1 disk of dough at a time, roll dough between 2 large sheets of parchment to ¼-inch thickness. (Keep second disk of dough refrigerated while rolling out first.) Peel off top parchment sheet and use 3½-inch cookie cutter to cut out cookies. Peel away scraps from around cookies and space cookies ¾ inch apart on prepared sheets. Repeat rolling and cutting steps with dough scraps. (If all cookies do not fit on sheets and second round of baking is required, let sheets cool completely before proceeding.)

4. Bake until cookies are puffy and just set around edges, 9 to 11 minutes, switching and rotating sheets halfway through baking. Let cookies cool on sheets for 10 minutes, then transfer to wire rack and let cool completely before decorating and serving.

decorating icing
makes 1⅓ cups
For colored icing, stir one or two drops of food coloring into the icing before transferring it to a pastry bag.

2 large egg whites

2⅔ cups (10⅔ ounces) confectioners' sugar

1. Using stand mixer fitted with whisk attachment, whip egg whites and sugar on medium-low speed until combined, about 1 minute. Increase speed to medium-high and whip until glossy, soft peaks form, 2 to 3 minutes, scraping down bowl as needed.

2. Transfer icing to pastry bag fitted with small round pastry tip. Decorate cookies and let icing harden before serving.

to make ahead
Wrapped dough can be refrigerated for up to 24 hours. Finished cookies can be stored with a sheet of parchment or waxed paper between each layer for up to 3 days.

biscochitos

why this recipe works Biscochitos are a New Mexican holiday tradition with Spanish roots. These crisp anise- and cinnamon-scented shortbread cookies traditionally get their tender texture from lard, but we achieved perfectly rich and tender results using the easier-to-find combination of butter and shortening. After chilling the dough to firm it up, we sliced these cookies into their signature diamond shape using a pizza cutter. For a crisp, sweet finish, we tossed the warm-from-the-oven cookies in cinnamon sugar so it adhered and then let the cookies cool completely before serving them. Grinding the anise seeds for this recipe is simple; just 10 seconds in a spice or coffee grinder pulverizes them to a powder. Don't let the cookies cool on the baking sheets longer than 5 minutes or the cinnamon sugar mixture won't adhere.

makes about 40 cookies
total time: 45 minutes
(plus 30 minutes for chilling)

1 cup (7 ounces) sugar

1 teaspoon ground cinnamon

1 tablespoon anise seeds

8 tablespoons unsalted butter, softened

8 tablespoons vegetable shortening, cut into 1-inch chunks

½ teaspoon salt

1 large egg yolk

1 teaspoon vanilla extract

2 cups (10 ounces) all-purpose flour

1. Line 2 baking sheets with parchment paper. Combine sugar and cinnamon in small bowl; reserve ½ cup cinnamon sugar in shallow dish. Grind anise seeds in spice grinder until finely ground, about 10 seconds.

2. Using stand mixer fitted with paddle, beat butter, shortening, salt, remaining ½ cup cinnamon sugar, and ground anise on medium-high speed until fluffy, about 3 minutes, scraping down bowl as needed. Add egg yolk and vanilla and mix until combined.

3. Reduce speed to low, add flour, and mix until dough forms, about 10 seconds. Place piece of parchment on counter; transfer dough to parchment and roll dough into 9-inch circle, about ½ inch thick. Transfer dough on parchment to large plate, cover with plastic wrap, and refrigerate until firm, about 30 minutes. Adjust oven racks to upper-middle and lower-middle positions and heat oven to 350 degrees.

4. Transfer dough, still on parchment, to cutting board. Using knife or pizza wheel, cut dough lengthwise into 1-inch-wide strips, then cut diagonally into 1-inch-wide strips to form diamonds. Space diamonds evenly on prepared sheets, about 20 per sheet.

5. Bake until set and just starting to brown, about 15 minutes, switching and rotating sheets halfway through baking. Let cookies cool on sheets for 5 minutes. Gently toss cookies, a few at a time, in reserved cinnamon sugar. Transfer cookies to wire racks and let cool completely.

chocolate pots de crème

why this recipe works Classic pots de crème can be finicky and laborious, requiring a hot water bath that threatens to splash the custards every time the pan is moved. We wanted a user-friendly recipe that delivered a decadent individual-size dessert with a satiny texture and intense chocolate flavor. Our boldest decision was to move the dish out of the oven, cooking the custard on the stovetop before pouring it into ramekins. A combination of heavy cream and half-and-half, along with egg yolks, gave us just the right amount of richness and body. For intense chocolate flavor, we focused on bittersweet chocolate—and a lot of it. The chocolate content was at least 50 percent more than in any other recipe we had encountered. We prefer pots de crème made with 60 percent bittersweet chocolate. Our favorite brands are Ghirardelli and Callebaut. Before whipping cream, chill the mixing bowl and whisk in the freezer for 20 minutes. To make chocolate shavings, simply shave bittersweet bar chocolate with a vegetable peeler.

serves 8
total time: 1 hour
(plus 4 hours for chilling)

pots de crème
10 ounces bittersweet chocolate, chopped fine

5 large egg yolks

5 tablespoons (2¼ ounces) sugar

¼ teaspoon salt

1½ cups heavy cream

¾ cup half-and-half

1 tablespoon water

½ teaspoon instant espresso powder

1 tablespoon vanilla extract

whipped cream and garnish
½ cup heavy cream, chilled

2 teaspoons sugar

½ teaspoon vanilla extract

Unsweetened cocoa powder (optional)

Chocolate shavings (optional)

1. for the pots de crème Place chocolate in medium bowl; set fine-mesh strainer over bowl and set aside.

2. Whisk egg yolks, sugar, and salt in bowl until combined. Whisk in cream and half-and-half. Transfer mixture to medium saucepan and cook over medium-low heat, stirring constantly and scraping bottom of pot with wooden spoon, until thickened and silky and registers 175 to 180 degrees, 8 to 12 minutes. (Do not let custard overcook or simmer.)

3. Immediately pour custard through fine-mesh strainer over chocolate. Let mixture stand to melt chocolate, about 5 minutes; whisk gently until smooth. Combine water and espresso powder and stir to dissolve, then whisk dissolved espresso powder and vanilla into chocolate mixture. Divide mixture evenly among eight 5-ounce ramekins. Gently tap ramekins against counter to remove air bubbles.

4. Let pots de crème cool to room temperature then cover with plastic wrap and refrigerate until chilled, at least 4 hours. Before serving, let pots de crème stand at room temperature for 20 to 30 minutes.

5. for the whipped cream and garnish Using handheld mixer or stand mixer fitted with whisk, whip cream, sugar, and vanilla on medium-low speed until foamy, about 1 minute. Increase speed to high and whip until soft peaks form, 1 to 3 minutes. Dollop each pot de crème with about 2 tablespoons whipped cream and garnish with cocoa and/or chocolate shavings, if using. Serve.

to make ahead
Pots de crème can be refrigerated for up to 3 days in step 4.

chocolate soufflé

why this recipe works Rising dramatically above the rim of the dish, this chocolate soufflé requires last-minute preparation, but with a texture that graduates from a crusty exterior to an airy outer layer to a rich, soft center, we think it's worth it. A base of egg yolks and sugar, beaten together until thick, created plenty of airy volume and allowed the rich flavor of the melted chocolate to take center stage. Beating and folding in two extra egg whites gave the soufflé even more lift and an even more ethereal texture. A soufflé waits for no one so be ready to serve it immediately. If you prefer to plan ahead and have individual ramekins on hand, our make-ahead variation makes this time-sensitive dessert possible for any occasion.

serves 6 to 8
total time: 1 hour

4 tablespoons unsalted butter, cut into ½-inch pieces, plus 1 tablespoon, softened

⅓ cup (2⅓ ounces) plus 1 tablespoon sugar

8 ounces bittersweet or semisweet chocolate, chopped coarse

1 tablespoon orange-flavored liqueur, such as Grand Marnier

½ teaspoon vanilla extract

⅛ teaspoon salt

6 large eggs, separated, plus 2 large whites

¼ teaspoon cream of tartar

1. Adjust oven rack to lower-middle position and heat oven to 375 degrees. Grease 2-quart soufflé dish with 1 tablespoon softened butter, then coat dish evenly with 1 tablespoon sugar; refrigerate until ready to use.

2. Melt chocolate and remaining 4 tablespoons butter in medium heatproof bowl set over saucepan filled with 1 inch of barely simmering water, making sure that water does not touch bottom of bowl, stirring occasionally, until smooth. Stir in liqueur, vanilla, and salt; set aside.

3. Using stand mixer fitted with paddle, beat egg yolks and remaining ⅓ cup sugar on medium speed until thick and pale yellow, about 3 minutes. Fold into chocolate mixture.

4. Using dry, clean bowl and whisk attachment, whip egg whites and cream of tartar on medium-low speed until foamy, about 1 minute. Increase speed to medium-high and whip until stiff peaks form, 3 to 4 minutes.

5. Using rubber spatula, vigorously stir one-quarter of whipped whites into chocolate mixture. Gently fold in remaining whites until just incorporated. Transfer mixture to prepared dish and bake until fragrant, fully risen, and exterior is set but interior is still a bit loose and creamy, about 25 minutes. (Use 2 large spoons to gently pull open top and peek inside.) Serve immediately.

variations

mocha soufflé

Add 1 tablespoon instant espresso powder dissolved in 1 tablespoon hot water when adding vanilla to chocolate mixture.

individual chocolate soufflés

Omit 2-quart soufflé dish. Grease eight 8-ounce ramekins with 1 tablespoon butter, then coat dishes evenly with 1 tablespoon sugar. In step 5, transfer soufflé mixture to ramekins, making sure to completely fill each ramekin and wipe rims with wet paper towel. Reduce baking time to 16 to 18 minutes. *(Makes 8 individual soufflés.)*

to make ahead

Omit 2-quart soufflé dish. Grease eight 8-ounce ramekins with 1 tablespoon butter, then coat dishes evenly with 1 tablespoon sugar. In step 3, bring remaining ⅓ cup sugar and 2 tablespoons water to boil in small saucepan, then reduce heat and simmer until sugar dissolves. With mixer running, slowly add sugar syrup to egg yolks and beat until mixture triples in volume, about 3 minutes. Whip egg whites as directed, beating in 2 tablespoons confectioners' sugar. Stir and fold into chocolate base as directed. Fill each ramekin almost to rim, wiping rims with wet paper towel. Cover each ramekin tightly with plastic wrap and freeze until firm, at least 3 hours or up to 1 month. (Do not thaw before baking.) Heat oven to 400 degrees and reduce baking time to 16 to 18 minutes. *(Makes 8 individual soufflés.)*

classic lemon tart

why this recipe works The tart sweetness of this sunny, elegant lemon tart offers a bright spot in any holiday meal, one that is especially welcome in the cold winter months. The success of the tart hinges on creating the perfect lemon curd. For just enough sweetness to offset the supertart lemons, we used 3 parts sugar to 2 parts lemon juice, plus a whopping ¼ cup of lemon zest. To achieve a curd that was creamy and dense in a vibrant, lemony yellow, we used a combination of whole eggs and egg yolks. We cooked the curd over direct heat and then whisked in the butter. For a smooth, light texture, we strained the curd, and we stirred in heavy cream just before baking. Poured into a buttery, sturdy prebaked tart shell, this simple curd created just the smooth, sweet-tart dessert we wanted. Once the lemon curd ingredients have been combined, cook the curd immediately; otherwise, it will have a grainy finished texture. The shell should still be warm when the filling is added. Dust with confectioners' sugar before serving, or serve with Whipped Cream.

serves 8 to 10
total time: 30 minutes
(plus 2 hours for cooling)

2 large eggs plus 7 large yolks

1 cup (7 ounces) sugar

¼ cup grated lemon zest plus ⅔ cup juice (4 lemons)

Pinch salt

4 tablespoons unsalted butter, cut into 4 pieces

3 tablespoons heavy cream

1 recipe Classic Tart Dough (page 158), fully baked and still warm

1. Adjust oven rack to middle position and heat oven to 375 degrees. Whisk eggs and yolks together in medium saucepan. Whisk in sugar until combined, then whisk in lemon zest and juice and salt. Add butter and cook over medium-low heat, stirring constantly, until mixture thickens slightly and registers 170 degrees, about 5 minutes. Immediately pour mixture through fine-mesh strainer into bowl and stir in cream.

2. Pour warm lemon filling into warm prebaked tart shell. Bake tart on baking sheet until filling is shiny and opaque and center jiggles slightly when shaken, 10 to 15 minutes, rotating baking sheet halfway through baking. Transfer tart with baking sheet to wire rack and let cool to room temperature, about 2 hours. To serve, remove outer metal ring of tart pan, slide thin metal spatula between tart and tart pan bottom, and carefully slide tart onto serving platter or cutting board.

whipped cream
makes about 2 cups
For lightly sweetened whipped cream, reduce sugar to 1½ teaspoons. Chill the mixer bowl and whisk in the freezer for 20 minutes before whipping the cream.

1 cup heavy cream, chilled

1 tablespoon sugar

1 teaspoon vanilla extract

Using stand mixer fitted with whisk, whip cream, sugar, and vanilla on medium-low speed until foamy, about 1 minute. Increase speed to high and whip until soft peaks form, 1 to 3 minutes.

to make ahead
Tart can be held at room temperature for up to 6 hours. Whipped cream can be transferred to fine-mesh strainer set over small bowl, covered with plastic wrap, and refrigerated for up to 8 hours.

baked raspberry tart

why this recipe works Tart raspberries, rich custard, and a buttery crust are a classic white-tablecloth combination. Our version is perfect for a special occasion, offering a more casual, rustic approach to that perfect marriage of fruit, custard, and pastry. We started with a simple butter, egg, sugar, and flour batter, heightening its flavor by browning the butter instead of simply melting it. Lemon zest brightened the custardy filling and fruity kirsch contributed a sophisticated accent. Using one whole egg plus an egg white ensured that the filling would set into a nicely firm yet creamy texture. Substituting instant flour for all-purpose produced an effortlessly smooth and silky (rather than starchy) texture. We arranged the raspberries in the bottom of our favorite tart shell and poured in the filling. The filling baked up golden brown, loaded with sweet-tart berries, and bound to please every guest at the table. Wondra is an instant flour sold in canisters in the baking aisle. To minimize waste, reserve the egg white left from making the tart pastry for use in the filling. If your raspberries are very tart or very sweet, adjust the amount of sugar in the filling by about a tablespoon or so. The tart is best eaten the day it is made.

serves 8 to 10
total time: 1 hour
(plus 2 hours for cooling)

6 tablespoons unsalted butter

1 large egg plus 1 large white

½ cup (3½ ounces) plus 1 tablespoon sugar

¼ teaspoon salt

1 teaspoon vanilla extract

1 teaspoon kirsch or framboise (optional)

¼ teaspoon grated lemon zest plus 1½ teaspoons juice

2 tablespoons Wondra flour

2 tablespoons heavy cream

1 recipe Classic Tart Dough (page 158), partially baked and cooled

10 ounces (2 cups) raspberries

1. Adjust oven rack to middle position and heat oven to 375 degrees. Melt butter in small saucepan over medium heat, swirling occasionally, until butter is browned and releases nutty aroma, about 7 minutes. Transfer butter to small bowl and let cool slightly. Whisk egg and egg white in medium bowl until combined. Add sugar and salt and whisk vigorously until light colored, about 1 minute. Whisk in warm browned butter until combined, then whisk in vanilla; kirsch, if using; and lemon zest and juice. Whisk in Wondra, then whisk in cream until combined.

2. Distribute raspberries in single tightly packed layer in bottom of cooled prebaked tart shell. Pour filling mixture evenly over raspberries. Bake tart on baking sheet until fragrant and filling is set (it does not jiggle when shaken), bubbling lightly around edges, and surface is puffed and deep golden brown, about 30 minutes, rotating sheet halfway through baking. Transfer tart with baking sheet to wire rack and let cool to room temperature, about 2 hours. To serve, remove outer metal ring of tart pan, slide thin metal spatula between tart and tart pan bottom, and carefully slide tart onto serving platter or cutting board.

variations

baked blackberry tart
Substitute 10 ounces blackberries for raspberries.

baked blueberry-raspberry tart
Replace 5 ounces raspberries with 5 ounces blueberries.

to make ahead
Baked and cooled tart can be wrapped loosely with plastic wrap and held at room temperature for up to 4 hours before serving.

quick tarte tatin with pears

why this recipe works While a true tarte Tatin requires an investment of time and a certain amount of skill, our pared-down version promises deeply caramelized fruit and buttery pastry in a fraction of the time, making it the perfect dessert for the time-pressed holiday host. We first baked a sheet of store-bought puff pastry until it was beautifully golden brown. While the pastry baked, we caramelized pears in a skillet until they were tender. We then arranged the pears over the pastry in rows that put their deeply browned edges on full display. To reinforce the fruit's darkly sweet, caramelized flavor, we drizzled the pears in a sweet, boozy sauce made by adding heavy cream and Poire William to the juices left behind in the skillet. To get this dessert on the table in under an hour, peel the pears while the oven preheats and the pastry thaws, and then bake the pastry while the pears are caramelizing. We like to use Bosc or Bartlett pears here because they maintain their shape nicely when cooked. To thaw frozen puff pastry, let it sit either in the refrigerator for 24 hours or on the counter for 30 minutes to 1 hour. We like this sauce with Poire William (or other pear liqueur) but Grand Marnier will also work. Serve with Tangy Whipped Cream.

serves 6 to 8
total time: 30 minutes

1 (9½ by 9-inch) sheet frozen puff pastry, thawed

8 tablespoons unsalted butter

¾ cup (5¼ ounces) sugar

2 pounds Bosc or Bartlett pears, peeled, quartered, and cored

¼ cup heavy cream

2 tablespoons Poire William (optional)

1. Adjust oven rack to middle position and heat oven to 400 degrees. Line rimmed baking sheet with parchment paper. Unfold puff pastry, lay on prepared baking sheet, and bake until golden brown and puffed, 15 to 20 minutes, rotating baking sheet halfway through. Transfer baked pastry sheet to serving platter and press lightly to flatten if domed.

2. Meanwhile, melt butter in 12-inch nonstick skillet over high heat. Remove pan from heat and sprinkle evenly with sugar. Lay pears in skillet, return skillet to high heat, and cook until juice in pan turns rich amber color and pears are caramelized, 20 to 25 minutes, turning pears halfway through cooking.

3. Remove pears from pan one at a time and arrange in 3 overlapping rows on baked pastry sheet, leaving ½-inch border. Spoon about half of pan juice over pears.

4. Whisk cream and Poire William (if using) into remaining juice in pan and bring to simmer. Pour some sauce over tart and serve, passing remaining sauce separately.

variation

quick tarte tatin with apples
Substitute 2 pounds Granny Smith apples (about 4 large) for pears and Grand Marnier, spiced rum, or Calvados for Poire William. Start checking apples for doneness in step 2 after 15 to 20 minutes.

tangy whipped cream
makes 1½ cups
Chill the mixer bowl and whisk in the freezer for 20 minutes before whipping the cream.

1 cup heavy cream, chilled

¼ cup sour cream, chilled

¼ cup packed (1¾ ounces) light brown sugar

⅛ teaspoon vanilla extract

Using stand mixer fitted with whisk, whip all ingredients together on medium-low speed until foamy, about 1 minute. Increase speed to high and whip until soft peaks form, 1 to 3 minutes.

to make ahead
Baked tart can be held at room temperature for up to 30 minutes before serving.

deep-dish apple pie

why this recipe works There's no better way to enjoy fall's abundant apple harvest than in a towering deep-dish pie. Unfortunately, this dessert often yields unevenly cooked, shrunken apples swimming in an ocean of their own exuded juices atop a pale, soggy crust. We wanted each slice to be dense with juicy apples, framed by a buttery, flaky crust. A combination of sweet and tart apples, tossed with a little brown sugar, salt, lemon, and cinnamon, promised a perfectly balanced filling. Precooking the apples solved the shrinking problem, helping them hold their shape in the oven while also eliminating any excess liquid, and thereby protecting the bottom crust. We mounded the cooled slices in our pie plate, covered them in the top crust, and baked. Our sky-high apple pie emerged golden brown and chock-full of tender apples, filling our kitchen with the homey, comforting aromas of this autumn favorite. Good choices for tart apples are Granny Smiths, Empires, or Cortlands; for sweet we recommend Golden Delicious, Jonagolds, or Braeburns. Serve with vanilla ice cream.

serves 8
total time: 1 hour
(plus 3 hours for
chilling and cooling)

1 recipe Basic Double-Crust Pie Dough (page 159)

2½ pounds firm tart apples (about 5 large), peeled, cored, and sliced ¼ inch thick

2½ pounds firm sweet apples (about 5 large), peeled, cored, and sliced ¼ inch thick

½ cup (3½ ounces) plus 1 tablespoon granulated sugar

¼ cup packed (1¾ ounces) light brown sugar

½ teaspoon grated lemon zest plus 1 tablespoon juice

¼ teaspoon salt

⅛ teaspoon ground cinnamon

1 large egg white, lightly beaten

1. Roll 1 disk of dough into 12-inch circle on lightly floured work surface, then fit into 9-inch pie plate, letting excess dough hang over edge; cover with plastic wrap and refrigerate for 30 minutes. Roll other disk of dough into 12-inch circle on lightly floured work surface, then transfer to parchment-lined baking sheet; cover with plastic wrap and refrigerate for 30 minutes.

2. Toss apples, ½ cup granulated sugar, brown sugar, lemon zest, salt, and cinnamon together in Dutch oven. Cover and cook over medium heat, stirring frequently, until apples are tender when poked with fork but still hold their shape, 15 to 20 minutes. Transfer apples and their juice to rimmed baking sheet and let cool to room temperature, about 30 minutes.

3. Adjust oven rack to lowest position and heat oven to 425 degrees. Drain cooled apples thoroughly in colander set over bowl, reserving ¼ cup juice. Stir lemon juice into reserved ¼ cup apple juice.

4. Spread apples into dough-lined pie plate, mounding them slightly in middle, and drizzle with lemon juice mixture. Loosely roll second piece of dough around rolling pin and gently unroll it over pie. Trim, fold, and crimp edges and cut 4 vent holes in top. Brush dough with egg white and sprinkle with remaining 1 tablespoon sugar.

5. Place pie on rimmed baking sheet and bake until crust is golden, about 25 minutes. Reduce oven temperature to 375 degrees, rotate sheet, and continue to bake until juices are bubbling and crust is deep golden brown, 30 to 40 minutes longer. Let pie cool on wire rack until filling has set, about 2 hours; serve slightly warm or at room temperature.

to make ahead
Baked pie can be held at room temperature for up to 8 hours or refrigerated for up to 24 hours; to serve, refresh in 350 degree oven for 10 to 15 minutes (note: crust will soften). Unbaked pie (through step 4) can be frozen for up to 2 weeks. Freeze pie until firm, then wrap in double layer of plastic wrap followed by aluminum foil. Finish and bake pie as directed in step 5 (do not thaw), increasing baking time at 375 degrees to 40 to 50 minutes.

classic pecan pie

why this recipe works There is much to love about sweet, nutty pecan pie, but it's easy for this simple dessert to turn out toothachingly sugary and void of pecan flavor, with a curdled filling sogging a leathery crust. We wanted to create the ideal recipe for a not-too-sweet pie with a smooth-textured filling and a properly baked bottom crust. We decided to start from the bottom up. By partially baking the crust, we ensured that the filling wouldn't compromise its texture during baking and serving; we also found that adding the filling while the crust was still warm helped a great deal. Next, we melted the butter and stirred together the filling in a bowl set over almost-simmering water. This makeshift double-boiler setup helped us maintain gentle heat, which protected against curdling. We reversed the filling's sugar overload by using a moderate amount of brown sugar. Its subtle, nuanced sweetness and molasses taste kept the spotlight trained on the pecans' toasty flavor. Poured into the warm shell and baked to nutty perfection, this pecan pie moved right to the top of our nice list. Chill the dough-lined pie plate for at least 30 minutes before beginning the recipe. The crust must still be warm when the filling is added. To serve the pie warm, cool it thoroughly so that it sets, then warm it in a 250-degree oven for about 15 minutes and slice. Serve with vanilla ice cream or Whipped Cream (lightly sweetened, page 147).

serves 8
total time: 1 hour
(plus 2 hours for cooling)

1 recipe Basic Single-Crust Pie Dough (page 159), fitted into a 9-inch pie plate and chilled

6 tablespoons unsalted butter, cut into 1-inch pieces

1 cup packed (7 ounces) dark brown sugar

½ teaspoon salt

3 large eggs

¾ cup light corn syrup

1 tablespoon vanilla extract

2 cups (8 ounces) pecans, toasted and chopped fine

1. Adjust oven rack to middle position and heat oven to 375 degrees. Line chilled pie shell with double layer of foil and fill with pie weights. Bake until pie dough looks dry and is light in color, 25 to 30 minutes. Transfer pie plate to wire rack and remove weights and foil. Adjust oven rack to lower-middle position and reduce oven temperature to 275 degrees. (Crust must still be warm when filling is added.)

2. Melt butter in heatproof bowl set in skillet of water maintained at just below simmer. Remove bowl from skillet and stir in sugar and salt until butter is absorbed. Whisk in eggs, then corn syrup and vanilla until smooth. Return bowl to hot water and stir until mixture is shiny, hot to touch, and registers 130 degrees. Off heat, stir in pecans.

3. Pour pecan mixture into warm pie crust. Bake pie until filling looks set but yields when gently pressed with back of spoon, 50 minutes to 1 hour. Let pie cool on wire rack until filling has firmed up, about 2 hours; serve slightly warm (see note) or at room temperature.

to make ahead
Baked and cooled pie can be covered loosely with plastic wrap and refrigerated for up to 24 hours. Let pie come to room temperature before serving or, to serve warm, reheat pie in 300-degree oven for about 15 minutes.

pumpkin pie

why this recipe works Our pumpkin pie presents a new standard: velvety smooth, packed with pumpkin flavor, and perfectly spiced. Canned pumpkin contains flavor-diluting moisture, so we cooked the puree with sugar and spices to concentrate its taste and whisked in heavy cream, milk, and eggs to enrich it. Working with a hot filling helped the custard firm up quickly in the oven, preventing it from soaking into the crust. For spices, we used nutmeg, cinnamon, and, surprisingly, freshly grated ginger. Sugar and maple syrup sweetened things, but the addition of candied yams, mashed into the hot filling, really put our pie's flavor over the top. Starting the pie in a hot oven and then dropping the temperature partway through baking prevented curdling and cut the baking time to less than 1 hour. If candied yams are unavailable, regular canned yams can be substituted. When the pie is properly baked, the center 2 inches of the pie should look firm but jiggle slightly. The pie finishes cooking with residual heat; to ensure that the filling sets, cool it at room temperature and not in the refrigerator. Chill dough-lined pie plate for at least 30 minutes before beginning recipe. The crust and filling must both be warm when the filling is added. Serve with Whipped Cream (lightly sweetened, page 147).

serves 8
total time: 1 hour
(plus 2 hours for cooling)

1 recipe Basic Single-Crust Pie Dough (page 159), fitted into a 9-inch pie plate and chilled

1 cup heavy cream

1 cup whole milk

3 large eggs plus 2 large yolks

1 teaspoon vanilla extract

1 (15-ounce) can pumpkin puree

1 cup candied yams, drained

¾ cup (5¼ ounces) sugar

¼ cup maple syrup

2 teaspoons grated fresh ginger

1 teaspoon salt

½ teaspoon ground cinnamon

¼ teaspoon ground nutmeg

1. Adjust oven rack to middle position and heat oven to 375 degrees. Line chilled pie shell with double layer of foil and fill with pie weights.

2. Bake until pie dough looks dry and is light in color, 25 to 30 minutes. Remove weights and foil and continue to bake crust until deep golden brown, 10 to 12 minutes longer. Transfer pie plate to wire rack. (Crust must still be warm when filling is added.)

3. While pie shell is baking, whisk cream, milk, eggs and yolks, and vanilla together in medium bowl. Bring pumpkin puree, yams, sugar, maple syrup, ginger, salt, cinnamon, and nutmeg to simmer in large saucepan over medium heat and cook, stirring constantly and mashing yams against sides of pot, until thick and shiny, 15 to 20 minutes.

4. Remove pan from heat and whisk in cream mixture until fully incorporated. Strain mixture through fine-mesh strainer set over medium bowl, using back of ladle or spatula to press solids through strainer. Whisk mixture, then transfer to warm prebaked pie crust.

5. Bake pie on rimmed baking sheet for 10 minutes. Reduce oven temperature to 300 degrees and continue to bake until edges of pie are set and center registers 175 degrees, 25 to 45 minutes longer, rotating sheet halfway through baking. Let pie cool on wire rack to room temperature, 2 to 3 hours, before serving.

to make ahead
Baked and cooled pie can be covered loosely with plastic wrap and refrigerated for up to 24 hours. Let pie come to room temperature before serving or, to serve warm, reheat pie in 300-degree oven for about 15 minutes.

classic tart dough

why this recipe works Tart crust should be fine-textured, buttery-rich, crisp, and crumbly. To reliably meet all these expectations, we used a full stick of butter for dough that tasted great and was easy to handle, yet still had a delicate crumb, and confectioners' sugar and all-purpose flour gave us a crisp texture. Our recipe yields enough dough to easily fit into a tart pan with enough extra to patch any holes.

makes enough for one 9-inch tart
total time: 1 hour
(plus 2 to 3 hours for chilling)

1 large egg yolk

1 tablespoon heavy cream

½ teaspoon vanilla extract

1¼ cups (6¼ ounces) all-purpose flour

⅔ cup (2⅔ ounces) confectioners' sugar

¼ teaspoon salt

8 tablespoons unsalted butter, cut into ¼-inch pieces and chilled

1. Whisk egg yolk, cream, and vanilla together in bowl. Process flour, sugar, and salt in food processor until combined, about 5 seconds. Scatter butter over top and pulse until mixture resembles coarse cornmeal, about 15 pulses. With machine running, add egg mixture and continue to process until dough just comes together around processor blade, about 12 seconds.

2. Turn dough onto sheet of plastic wrap and flatten into 6-inch disk. Wrap tightly in plastic and refrigerate for 1 hour. Before rolling dough out, let it sit on counter to soften slightly, about 10 minutes.

3. Roll dough into 11-inch circle on lightly floured counter (if at any point dough becomes too soft and sticky to work with, slip dough onto baking sheet and freeze or refrigerate until workable). Place dough round on baking sheet, cover with plastic, and refrigerate for about 30 minutes.

4. Remove dough from refrigerator; discard plastic but keep dough on baking sheet. Loosely roll dough around rolling pin and gently unroll it onto 9-inch tart pan with removable bottom, letting excess dough hang over edge. Ease dough into pan by gently lifting edge of dough with your hand while pressing into corners with your other hand. Leave any dough that overhangs pan in place.

5. Press dough into fluted sides of pan, forming distinct seam around pan's circumference. (If some sections of edge are too thin, reinforce them by folding excess dough back on itself.) Run rolling pin over top of tart pan to remove any excess dough. Wrap dough-lined tart pan loosely in plastic, place on large plate, and freeze until dough is fully chilled and firm, about 30 minutes, before using.

6. Adjust oven rack to middle position and heat oven to 375 degrees. Set dough-lined tart pan on rimmed baking sheet. Spray 1 side of double layer of aluminum foil with vegetable oil spray. Press foil greased side down into frozen tart shell, covering edges to prevent burning, and fill with pie weights.

7a. for a partially baked shell
Bake until tart shell is golden brown and set, about 30 minutes, rotating pan halfway through baking. Transfer tart shell with baking sheet to wire rack and carefully remove weights and foil. Use crust while it is still warm or let it cool completely (see individual tart recipe instructions).

7b. for a fully baked shell
Bake until tart shell is golden brown and set, about 30 minutes, rotating pan halfway through baking. Carefully remove weights and foil and continue to bake tart shell until it is fully baked and golden, 5 to 10 minutes longer. Transfer tart shell with baking sheet to wire rack and let tart shell cool completely, about 1 hour.

to make ahead
Dough can be wrapped tightly in plastic wrap and refrigerated for up to 2 days or frozen for up to 1 month. If frozen, let dough thaw completely on counter before rolling it out. Dough-lined tart pan can be wrapped tightly in plastic and frozen for up to 1 month.

basic pie dough

why this recipe works We wanted pie dough that we could count on for reliably flaky, flavorful, crust and achieving it came down to determining the right fat, the right proportion of fat to flour, and the right method for combining them. A proportion of 3 parts butter to 2 parts shortening proved optimal for both flavor and texture, and a high-fat ratio of 2 parts flour to 1 part fat produced a workable, tender dough.

makes enough for one 9-inch pie
total time: 30 minutes
(plus 1 hour for chilling)

basic single-crust pie dough

1¼ cups (6¼ ounces) all-purpose flour

1 tablespoon sugar

½ teaspoon salt

3 tablespoons vegetable shortening, cut into ½-inch pieces and chilled

5 tablespoons unsalted butter, cut into ¼-inch pieces and chilled

4–6 tablespoons ice water

1. Process flour, sugar, and salt in food processor until combined. Scatter shortening over top and process until mixture resembles coarse cornmeal, about 10 seconds. Scatter butter pieces over top and pulse until mixture resembles coarse crumbs, about 10 pulses. Transfer mixture to medium bowl.

2. Sprinkle 4 tablespoons ice water over mixture. Stir and press dough together, using stiff rubber spatula, until dough sticks together. If dough does not come together, stir in remaining water, 1 tablespoon at a time, until it does.

3. Turn dough onto sheet of plastic wrap and flatten into 4-inch disk. Wrap dough tightly in plastic wrap and refrigerate for 1 hour. Before rolling dough out, let sit on counter to soften slightly, about 10 minutes.

basic double-crust pie dough

2½ cups (12½ ounces) all-purpose flour

2 tablespoons sugar

1 teaspoon salt

½ cup vegetable shortening, cut into ½-inch pieces and chilled

12 tablespoons unsalted butter, cut into ¼-inch pieces and chilled

6–8 tablespoons ice water

1. Process flour, sugar, and salt in food processor until combined. Scatter shortening over top and process until mixture resembles coarse cornmeal, about 10 seconds. Scatter butter pieces over top and pulse until mixture resembles coarse crumbs, about 10 pulses. Transfer mixture to large bowl.

2. Sprinkle 6 tablespoons ice water over mixture. Stir and press dough together, using stiff rubber spatula, until dough sticks together. If dough does not come together, stir in remaining water, 1 tablespoon at a time, until it does.

3. Divide dough into 2 even pieces. Turn each piece of dough onto sheet of plastic wrap and flatten each into 4-inch disk. Wrap each piece tightly in plastic wrap and refrigerate for 1 hour. Before rolling dough out, let sit on counter to soften slightly, about 10 minutes.

variation

hand-mixed basic pie dough

Freeze butter in stick form until very firm. Whisk flour, sugar, and salt together in medium bowl. Add chilled shortening and press into the flour using fork. Grate frozen butter on large holes of box grater into flour mixture, then cut mixture together using 2 knives until mixture resembles coarse crumbs. Follow recipe for Basic Single-Crust Pie Dough or Basic Double-Crust Pie Dough, adding water as directed.

to make ahead

Dough can be wrapped tightly in plastic wrap and refrigerated for up to 2 days or frozen for up to 1 month. If frozen, let dough thaw completely on counter before rolling it out.

tiramisù

serves 10 to 12
total time: 45 minutes
(plus 6 hours for chilling)

why this recipe works From its boozy, coffee-soaked ladyfingers to its sweet, creamy filling, it's no wonder tiramisù is Italian for "pick me up." This invigorating dessert lives up to its name, especially when served at the end of an indulgent holiday feast. Our streamlined approach puts tiramisù's luxurious flavors and textures center stage. Instead of making a fussy custard-based filling, we simply whipped egg yolks, sugar, salt, rum, and mascarpone together. Whipped cream lightened the filling. We briefly moistened the ladyfingers in a mixture of coffee, espresso powder, and more rum. We prefer a tiramisù with a pronounced rum flavor; for a less potent rum flavor, reduce the amount of rum in the coffee mixture. Brandy and even whiskey can be substituted for the dark rum. Do not let the mascarpone warm to room temperature before whipping, or it might break. Dried ladyfingers are also called *savoiardi*; you will need between 42 and 60 savoiardi, depending on their size and brand.

2½ cups strong brewed coffee, room temperature

1½ tablespoons instant espresso powder

9 tablespoons dark rum

6 large egg yolks

⅔ cup (3⅓ ounces) sugar

¼ teaspoon salt

1½ pounds mascarpone, chilled

¾ cup heavy cream, chilled

14 ounces dried ladyfingers (savoiardi)

3½ tablespoons Dutch-processed cocoa powder

¼ cup grated semisweet or bittersweet chocolate (optional)

1. Stir coffee, espresso, and 5 tablespoons rum in wide bowl or baking dish until espresso dissolves.

2. Using stand mixer with whisk attachment, beat yolks at low speed until just combined.

Add sugar and salt and beat at medium-high speed until pale yellow, 1½ to 2 minutes, scraping down bowl as needed. Reduce speed to medium, add remaining 4 tablespoons rum, and beat at medium speed until just combined, 20 to 30 seconds; scrape bowl. Add mascarpone and beat until no lumps remain, 30 to 45 seconds, scraping down bowl as needed. Transfer mixture to large bowl.

3. In now-empty mixer bowl, beat cream at medium speed until frothy, 1 to 1½ minutes. Increase speed to high and continue to beat until cream holds stiff peaks, 1 to 1½ minutes. Using rubber spatula, fold one-third of whipped cream into mascarpone mixture to lighten, then gently fold in remaining whipped cream until no white streaks remain.

4. Working with 1 cookie at a time, drop half of ladyfingers into coffee mixture, roll, remove, and transfer to 13 by 9-inch baking dish. (Do not submerge ladyfingers in coffee mixture; entire process should take no longer than 2 to 3 seconds for

each cookie.) Arrange soaked ladyfingers in single layer in baking dish, breaking or trimming as needed to fit neatly into dish.

5. Spread half of mascarpone mixture over ladyfingers, spreading it to sides and into corners of dish, and smooth top. Place 2 tablespoons cocoa in fine-mesh strainer and dust cocoa over mascarpone.

6. Repeat with remaining ladyfingers, mascarpone, and 1½ tablespoons cocoa to make second layer. Clean edges of dish, cover with plastic wrap, and refrigerate until set, at least 6 hours. Before serving, sprinkle with grated chocolate, if using.

to make ahead
Tiramisù can be refrigerated for up to 24 hours or frozen for up to 1 month; if frozen, thaw completely in refrigerator before serving.

flourless chocolate cake

why this recipe works Rich with deep, intense chocolate flavor, flourless chocolate cake makes for a decadent conclusion to any meal, but most recipes require complicated techniques to get it on the table. Our take on this indulgent dessert minimizes fuss without sacrificing flavor or texture. We began by gently melting chocolate and butter in the microwave before incorporating the remaining ingredients. In the absence of flour, we called on eggs for structure, cornstarch for body, and water for a moist, smooth texture. Vanilla and espresso powder profoundly deepened the chocolate's impact. Ensuring a crack-free surface was as easy as straining and resting the batter, and then tapping out bubbles that rose to the surface. Baking in a low oven produced a perfectly smooth surface. This cake needs to chill for at least 6 hours, so we recommend making it the day before serving. An accurate oven thermometer is essential here. We prefer this cake made with 60 percent bittersweet chocolate. Our favorite brands are Ghirardelli and Callebaut. Before making whipped cream, chill the mixer bowl and whisk in the freezer for 20 minutes. Top the cake with chocolate shavings, if desired; to make shavings, shave bittersweet bar chocolate with a vegetable peeler.

serves 10 to 12
total time: 1 hour 30 minutes
(plus 7 hours for cooling and chilling)

cake
12 ounces bittersweet chocolate, broken into 1-inch pieces

16 tablespoons (2 sticks) unsalted butter

6 large eggs

1 cup (7 ounces) sugar

½ cup water

1 tablespoon cornstarch

1 tablespoon vanilla extract

1 teaspoon instant espresso powder

½ teaspoon salt

whipped cream
½ cup heavy cream, chilled

2 teaspoons sugar

½ teaspoon vanilla extract

1. for the cake Adjust oven rack to middle position and heat oven to 275 degrees. Spray 9-inch springform pan with vegetable oil spray. Microwave chocolate and butter in bowl at 50 percent power, stirring occasionally with rubber spatula, until melted, about 4 minutes. Let chocolate mixture cool for 5 minutes.

2. Whisk eggs, sugar, water, cornstarch, vanilla, espresso powder, and salt in large bowl until thoroughly combined, about 30 seconds. Whisk in chocolate mixture until smooth and slightly thickened, about 45 seconds. Strain batter through fine-mesh strainer into prepared pan, pressing against strainer with rubber spatula or back of ladle to help batter pass through.

3. Gently tap pan on counter to release air bubbles; then let sit on counter for 10 minutes to allow air bubbles to rise to top. Use tines of fork to gently pop any air bubbles that have risen to surface. Bake until edges are set and center jiggles slightly when cake is shaken gently, 45 to 50 minutes. Let cake cool for 5 minutes, then run paring knife between cake and sides of pan.

4. Let cake cool on wire rack until barely warm, about 30 minutes. Cover cake tightly with plastic wrap, poke small hole in top, and refrigerate until cold and firmly set, at least 6 hours.

5. for the whipped cream Using stand mixer fitted with whisk, whip cream, sugar, and vanilla on medium-low speed until foamy, about 1 minute. Increase speed to high and whip until stiff peaks form, 1 to 3 minutes.

6. To unmold cake, remove sides and slide thin metal spatula between cake bottom and pan bottom to loosen, then slide cake onto serving platter. Let cake stand at room temperature for 30 minutes. Slice with warm, dry knife. Dollop slices with whipped cream and serve.

to make ahead
Cake must chill for at least 6 hours; we recommend making it the day before serving.

spiced pumpkin cheesecake

why this recipe works Spiced pumpkin is a well-trod flavor profile, but this cheesecake truly delivers on all fronts, from its clear pumpkin flavor and warm spices to its velvety yet firm texture. For a complementary crust, we spiced up a graham cracker crust with ginger, cinnamon, and cloves. Blotting the pumpkin with paper towels removed excess moisture, protecting the crust. Heavy cream added richness and white sugar (rather than brown) let the pumpkin really shine. Be sure to use unsweetened pumpkin puree.

serves 12
total time: 2 hours and 30 minutes
(plus 8 hours 15 minutes for cooling and chilling)

crust
9 whole graham crackers, broken into 1-inch pieces

3 tablespoons sugar

½ teaspoon ground ginger

½ teaspoon ground cinnamon

¼ teaspoon ground cloves

6 tablespoons unsalted butter, melted

filling
1⅓ cups (9⅓ ounces) sugar

1 teaspoon ground cinnamon

½ teaspoon ground ginger

½ teaspoon salt

¼ teaspoon ground nutmeg

¼ teaspoon ground cloves

¼ teaspoon ground allspice

1 (15-ounce) can unsweetened pumpkin puree

1½ pounds cream cheese, cut into chunks and softened

1 tablespoon vanilla extract

1 tablespoon lemon juice

5 large eggs, room temperature

1 cup heavy cream

1 tablespoon unsalted butter, melted

1. for the crust Adjust oven rack to lower-middle position and heat oven to 325 degrees. Pulse crackers, sugar, ginger, cinnamon, and cloves in food processor until finely ground, about 15 pulses. Transfer crumbs to bowl, drizzle with melted butter, and mix with rubber spatula until evenly moistened. Transfer crumbs to 9-inch springform pan and, using bottom of dry measuring cup, press crumbs evenly into pan bottom. Bake until browned around edges, about 15 minutes, rotating pan halfway through baking. Let crust cool completely on wire rack, about 30 minutes, then wrap outside of pan with two 18-inch square pieces of heavy-duty aluminum foil and set springform pan in roasting pan. Bring kettle of water to boil.

2. for the filling Whisk sugar, cinnamon, ginger, salt, nutmeg, cloves, and allspice together in small bowl. Spread pumpkin over rimmed baking sheet and pat dry with several sheets of paper towels.

3. Using stand mixer fitted with paddle, beat cream cheese on medium-low speed until smooth, about 1 minute. Scrape down bowl, then beat in half of sugar mixture until combined, about 1 minute. Repeat with remaining sugar mixture. Beat in vanilla, lemon juice, and pumpkin until combined, about 1 minute; scrape down bowl. Beat in eggs, one at a time, until combined, about 1 minute. Beat in cream until combined, about 1 minute. Give filling final stir by hand.

4. Being careful not to disturb crust, brush inside of pan with melted butter. Pour filling into prepared pan and smooth top with rubber spatula. Set roasting pan on oven rack and pour enough boiling water into roasting pan to come about halfway up sides of springform pan. Bake until cheesecake registers 150 degrees, about 1½ hours. Let cake cool in roasting pan for 45 minutes, then remove from water, discard foil, and set on wire rack; continue to let cool until barely warm, about 3 hours. Wrap with plastic wrap and refrigerate until cold, at least 3 hours.

5. To unmold, wrap wet, hot dish towel around springform pan and let stand for 1 minute. Remove sides of pan, slide thin metal spatula between crust and pan bottom to loosen, and slide cake onto serving platter. Let sit at room temperature for about 30 minutes before serving.

to make ahead
Cheesecake can be made up to 3 days in advance, but crust will lose crispness after 1 day.

gâteau breton with apricot filling

why this recipe works Hailing from France's Brittany coast, gâteau Breton is a simple yet stately cake, rich in butter with a dense yet tender crumb, making it the perfect understated dessert for a special occasion. To guarantee that the thick batter produced the proper crumb, we avoided incorporating too much air (thereby creating a fluffy texture) by creaming butter and sugar for only 3 minutes before adding the yolks and flour. Briefly freezing a layer of the batter in the cake pan made easy work of spreading on the bright apricot filling, and a second stint in the freezer firmed up the apricot-topped batter so we could cleanly apply the top layer. We strongly prefer the flavor of California apricots in the filling. Mediterranean or Turkish apricots can be used, but increase the amount of lemon juice to 2 tablespoons.

serves 8
total time: 2 hours
(plus 1 hour 30 minutes for chilling, freezing, and cooling)

filling
⅔ cup water

½ cup dried California apricots, chopped

⅓ cup (2⅓ ounces) sugar

1 tablespoon lemon juice

cake
16 tablespoons unsalted butter, softened

¾ cup plus 2 tablespoons (6⅛ ounces) sugar

6 large egg yolks (1 lightly beaten with 1 teaspoon water)

2 tablespoons dark rum

1 teaspoon vanilla extract

2 cups (10 ounces) all-purpose flour

½ teaspoon salt

1. for the filling Process water and apricots in blender until uniformly pureed, about 2 minutes. Transfer puree to 10-inch nonstick skillet and stir in sugar. Set skillet over medium heat and cook, stirring frequently, until puree has darkened slightly and rubber spatula leaves distinct trail when dragged across bottom of pan, 10 to 12 minutes. Transfer filling to bowl and stir in lemon juice. Refrigerate filling until cool to touch, about 15 minutes.

2. for the cake Adjust oven rack to lower-middle position and heat oven to 350 degrees. Grease 9-inch round cake pan.

3. Using stand mixer fitted with paddle, beat butter on medium-high speed until smooth and lightened in color, 1 to 2 minutes. Add sugar and continue to beat until pale and fluffy, about 3 minutes longer. Add 5 egg yolks, one at a time, and beat until combined. Scrape down bowl, add rum and vanilla, and mix until incorporated, about 1 minute. Reduce speed to low, add flour and salt, and mix until flour is just incorporated, about 30 seconds. Give batter final stir by hand.

4. Spoon half of batter into bottom of prepared pan. Using small offset spatula, spread batter into even layer. Freeze for 10 minutes.

5. Spread ½ cup filling in even layer over chilled batter, leaving ¾-inch border around edge (reserve remaining filling for another use). Freeze for 10 minutes.

6. Gently spread remaining batter over filling. Using offset spatula, carefully smooth top of batter. Brush with egg yolk wash. Using tines of fork, make light scores in surface of cake, spaced about 1½ inches apart, in diamond pattern, being careful not to score all the way to sides of pan. Bake until top is golden brown and edges of cake start to pull away from sides of pan, 45 to 50 minutes. Let cake cool in pan on wire rack for 30 minutes. Run paring knife between cake and sides of pan, remove cake from pan, and let cool completely on rack, about 1 hour. Cut into wedges and serve.

variation
gâteau breton with prune filling
Increase water to 1 cup, substitute 1 cup pitted prunes for apricots, and omit sugar. Bring water and prunes to simmer in small saucepan over medium heat. Reduce heat to medium-low and cook until all liquid is absorbed and prunes are very soft, 10 to 12 minutes. Remove saucepan from heat, add lemon juice, and stir with wooden spoon, pressing prunes against side of saucepan, until coarsely pureed. Chill filling in bowl and refrigerate until cool to touch, about 15 minutes.

bittersweet chocolate roulade

why this recipe works Much as it is a standout holiday dessert both for its looks and its rich layers of chocolate and cream, chocolate roulade can be a baker's nightmare—a hard-to-roll cake with a dry texture and a filling that won't stay put. We wanted a recipe that produced a cake with a velvety texture and deep flavor, a thick, lush filling, and a decadent icing. We used bitter- or semisweet chocolate for maximum chocolate flavor. Six eggs gave our cake great support and a combination of cocoa and flour provided further structure while boosting its flavor. We baked the cake in a large rimmed baking sheet, cooled it briefly in the pan, then unmolded it onto a kitchen towel rubbed with cocoa to prevent sticking. While the cake was still warm, we rolled it up with the towel inside, cooled it briefly, and then unrolled the cake—this gave the cake "muscle memory" so it could be easily re-rolled into the same shape. For the filling, we made an espresso-flavored cream with lush mascarpone. A complex dark chocolate ganache, made with bittersweet chocolate and cognac, served as the roulade's exterior icing. Rolled, iced, and sliced to reveal a dramatic creamy swirl, our roulade was at once classic and refreshingly modern. We suggest that you make the filling and ganache first, and then make the cake while the ganache is setting up. Or, if you prefer, the cake can be baked, filled, and rolled—but not iced—then wrapped in plastic wrap and refrigerated for up to 24 hours. If serving this cake in the style of a holiday yule log, make wood-grain striations in the ganache with a fork. The roulade is best served at room temperature.

serves 8 to 10
total time: 1 hour 45 minutes

6 ounces bittersweet or semisweet chocolate, chopped fine

2 tablespoons cold unsalted butter, cut into 2 pieces

2 tablespoons cold water

¼ cup Dutch-processed cocoa powder, sifted, plus 1 tablespoon for unmolding

¼ cup (1¼ ounces) all-purpose flour

⅛ teaspoon salt

6 large eggs, separated, room temperature

⅓ cup (2⅓ ounces) sugar

1 teaspoon vanilla extract

⅛ teaspoon cream of tartar

1 recipe Espresso-Mascarpone Cream (recipe follows)

1 recipe Dark Chocolate Ganache (recipe follows)

1. Adjust oven rack to upper-middle position and heat oven to 400 degrees. Spray 17½ by 12-inch rimmed baking sheet with vegetable oil spray, cover pan bottom with parchment paper, and spray parchment with vegetable oil spray; dust with flour and tap out excess.

2. Heat chocolate, butter, and water in small heatproof bowl set over saucepan filled with 1 inch barely simmering water, stirring occasionally until smooth. Set aside to cool slightly. Sift ¼ cup cocoa, flour, and salt together into small bowl and set aside.

continued

continued from page 169

3. In stand mixer fitted with whisk, beat egg yolks at medium-high speed until just combined, about 15 seconds. With mixer running, add half of sugar. Continue to beat, scraping down sides of bowl as necessary, until yolks are pale yellow and mixture falls in thick ribbon when whisk is lifted, about 8 minutes. Add vanilla and beat to combine, scraping down bowl once, about 30 seconds. Turn mixture into medium bowl.

4. Using clean, dry mixer bowl and whisk attachment, beat egg whites and cream of tartar at medium speed until foamy, about 30 seconds. With mixer running, add about 1 teaspoon more sugar; continue beating until soft peaks form, about 40 seconds. Gradually add remaining sugar and beat until egg whites are glossy and hold stiff peaks when whisk is lifted, about 1 minute longer. Do not overbeat.

5. Stir chocolate mixture into egg yolks. With rubber spatula, stir one-quarter of egg whites into chocolate mixture to lighten it. Fold in remaining egg whites until almost no streaks remain. Sprinkle cocoa-flour mixture over top and fold in quickly but gently.

6. Pour batter into prepared pan; using spatula and working quickly, even surface and smooth batter into pan corners. Lightly tap pan against countertop 2 or 3 times to settle batter. Bake until center of cake springs back when touched, 8 to 10 minutes, rotating pan halfway through baking time. Cool cake in pan on wire rack for 5 minutes.

7. While cake is cooling, lay clean dish towel over work surface and sift remaining 1 tablespoon cocoa over towel; rub cocoa into towel. Run small knife around baking sheet to loosen cake. Flip cake onto towel and peel off parchment.

8. Roll cake, towel and all, into jellyroll shape. Cool for 15 minutes, then unroll cake and towel. Using spatula, immediately spread filling evenly over cake, almost to edges. Roll up cake gently but snugly around filling. Set large sheet of parchment paper on overturned rimmed baking sheet and set roulade, seam side down, on top. Trim both ends on diagonal. Spread ganache evenly over roulade. Use fork to make wood-grain striations, if desired, on surface of ganache before icing has set. Refrigerate cake on baking sheet, uncovered, to slightly set icing, about 20 minutes.

9. Carefully slide two wide metal spatulas under cake and transfer cake to serving platter. Cut into slices and serve.

to make ahead
Cake can be baked, filled, and rolled—but not iced—then wrapped in plastic wrap and refrigerated for up to 24 hours.

espresso-mascarpone cream
makes about 2½ cups
Mascarpone is a fresh Italian cheese. It is sold in small containers in some supermarkets as well as most gourmet stores, cheese shops, and Italian markets.

½ cup heavy cream

2 teaspoons instant espresso powder or instant coffee powder

6 tablespoons confectioners' sugar (1½ ounces)

16½ ounces mascarpone cheese (generous 2 cups)

1. Bring cream to simmer in small saucepan over high heat. Off heat, stir in espresso and confectioners' sugar; cool slightly.

2. With spatula, beat mascarpone in medium bowl until softened. Gently whisk in cooled cream mixture until combined. Cover with plastic wrap and refrigerate until ready to use.

dark chocolate ganache

makes about 1½ cups
If your kitchen is cool and the ganache becomes too stiff to spread, set the bowl over a saucepan of simmering water, then stir briefly until it is smooth and icing-like.

¾ cup heavy cream

2 tablespoons unsalted butter

6 ounces bittersweet or semisweet chocolate, chopped

1 tablespoon cognac

Microwave cream and butter in microwave-safe measuring cup on high power until bubbling, about 1½ minutes. (Alternatively, bring to simmer in small saucepan over medium-high heat.) Place chocolate in food processor. With machine running, gradually add hot cream mixture and cognac through feed tube and process until smooth and thickened, about 3 minutes. Transfer ganache to medium bowl and let stand at room temperature for 1 hour, until spreadable (ganache should have consistency of soft icing).

assembling a roulade

1. Lay clean dish towel on counter. Immediately run knife around edge of cake, then flip hot cake onto towel. Discard parchment.

2. Roll cake—towel and all—into jelly roll shape. Cool for 15 minutes, then unroll cake and towel.

3. Using offset spatula, immediately spread filling evenly over surface of cake, almost to edges.

4. Roll cake up gently but snugly around filling.

5. Trim both ends on diagonal and spread ganache over roulade with small icing spatula.

6. If desired, use fork to make wood-grain striations on surface of ganache before icing has set. Slide 2 wide metal spatulas under cake to transfer to platter.

flavoring herbed roast turkey (page 36)

1. Rub herb paste under skin and directly onto flesh, distributing it evenly.

2. Make 1½-inch slit in each breast. Swing knife tip through breast, creating large pocket.

3. Apply layer of paste inside each pocket. Rub remaining paste inside turkey cavity and on skin.

halving cornish game hens (page 48)

1. Using kitchen shears and working with 1 hen at a time, with hen breast side down, cut through bones on either side of backbone; discard backbone.

2. Lay hens breast side up on counter. Using sharp chef's knife, cut through center of breast to make 2 halves.

seasoning slow-roasted fresh ham (page 52)

1. Cut pocket in meaty end and rub ham all over (including in pocket) with seasoning mixture.

2. Tie twine around base to create streamlined shape so ham cooks evenly.

stuffing herb-stuffed pork loin (page 57)

1. With fat side up, cut into loin two-thirds up from bottom, stopping ½ inch from edge. Peel back top flap and cut down, stopping ½ inch from bottom.

2. Cut back into thicker mass, again stopping ½ inch from edge. Open up loin, flatten, season, and refrigerate. Spread filling evenly over interior side, leaving ½-inch border on all sides.

3. Carefully roll roast, leaving fat side up. Tie at 1-inch intervals.

readying two roasts for porchetta (page 58)

1. After crosshatching surface, halve pork butt, creating two smaller roasts.

2. Cut deep slits into sides of roasts, then rub salt and herb paste over roasts and into slits.

3. Using 3 pieces of kitchen twine per roast, tie each roast into a compact cylinder.

trimming boneless rib roast (page 64)

1. Using sharp knife, trim fat cap to even ¼-inch thickness. Refrigerate trimmings.

2. Cut 1-inch crosshatch pattern into fat cap, being careful not to cut into meat.

3. Place 3 ounces of reserved trimmings in roasting pan (rendered fat will be used for Yorkshire pudding).

1. Remove kitchen twine used to hold legs together. Slice turkey through skin between leg and breast to expose the hip joint.

2. Pull leg quarters away from carcass. Separate joint by gently pressing leg out to side and pushing up on joint. Carefully cut through joint.

3. Cut through joint connecting drumstick to thigh on each side. Slice meat off drumsticks and thighs, leaving some skin attached to each slice.

4. Pull wings away from carcass and carefully cut through joint between wing and breast to remove wings. Cut wings in half for easier eating.

5. Cut down along 1 side following curvature of breastbone, pulling breast meat away from bone as you cut. Continue to cut and pry until breast has been removed.

6. Cut breast meat crosswise into thin slices for serving.

cooking lobster for lobster fettuccine with fennel and tarragon (page 75)

soft-shell	steaming time	meat yield	hard-shell	steaming time	meat yield
1 pound	8 to 9 minutes	about 3 ounces	1 pound	10 to 11 minutes	4 to 4½ ounces
1¼ pounds	11 to 12 minutes	3½ to 4 ounces	1¼ pounds	13 to 14 minutes	5½ to 6 ounces
1½ pounds	13 to 14 minutes	5½ to 6 ounces	1½ pounds	15 to 16 minutes	7½ to 8 ounces
1¾-2 pounds	17 to 18 minutes	6¼ to 6½ ounces	1¾-2 pounds	about 19 minutes	8½ to 9 ounces

conversions and equivalents

Some say cooking is a science and an art. We would say that geography has a hand in it, too. Flours and sugars manufactured in the United Kingdom and elsewhere will feel and taste different from those manufactured in the United States. So we cannot promise that the pie crust you bake in Canada or England will taste the same as a pie crust baked in the States, but we can offer guidelines for converting weights and measures. We also recommend that you rely on your instincts when making our recipes. Refer to the visual cues provided. If the pie dough hasn't "come together," as described, you may need to add more water—even if the recipe doesn't tell you to. You be the judge.

The recipes in this book were developed using standard U.S. measures following U.S. government guidelines. The charts below offer equivalents for U.S. and metric measures. All conversions are approximate and have been rounded up or down to the nearest whole number. For example:

$$1 \text{ teaspoon } = 4.9292 \text{ milliliters, rounded up to 5 milliliters}$$
$$1 \text{ ounce } = 28.3495 \text{ grams, rounded down to 28 grams}$$

volume conversions

u.s.	metric
1 teaspoon	5 milliliters
2 teaspoons	10 milliliters
1 tablespoon	15 milliliters
2 tablespoons	30 milliliters
¼ cup	59 milliliters
⅓ cup	79 milliliters
½ cup	118 milliliters
¾ cup	177 milliliters
1 cup	237 milliliters
1¼ cups	296 milliliters
1½ cups	355 milliliters
2 cups (1 pint)	473 milliliters
2½ cups	591 milliliters
3 cups	710 milliliters
4 cups (1 quart)	0.946 liter
1.06 quarts	1 liter
4 quarts (1 gallon)	3.8 liters

weight conversions

ounces	grams
½	14
¾	21
1	28
1½	43
2	57
2½	71
3	85
3½	99
4	113
4½	128
5	142
6	170
7	198
8	227
9	255
10	283
12	340
16 (1 pound)	454

conversion for common baking ingredients

Baking is an exacting science. Because measuring by weight is far more accurate than measuring by volume, and thus more likely to produce reliable results, in our recipes we provide ounce measures in addition to cup measures for many ingredients. Refer to the chart below to convert these measures into grams.

ingredient	ounces	grams
flour		
1 cup all-purpose flour*	5	142
1 cup cake flour	4	113
1 cup whole-wheat flour	5½	156
sugar		
1 cup granulated (white) sugar	7	198
1 cup packed brown sugar (light or dark)	7	198
1 cup confectioners' sugar	4	113
cocoa powder		
1 cup cocoa powder	3	85
butter†		
4 tablespoons (½ stick, or ¼ cup)	2	57
8 tablespoons (1 stick, or ½ cup)	4	113
16 tablespoons (2 sticks, or 1 cup)	8	227

* *U.S. all-purpose flour, the most frequently used flour in this book, does not contain leaveners, as some European flours do. These leavened flours are called self-rising or self-raising. If you are using self-rising flour, take this into consideration before adding leavening to a recipe.*

† *In the United States, butter is sold both salted and unsalted. We generally recommend unsalted butter. If you are using salted butter, take this into consideration before adding salt to a recipe.*

oven temperatures

fahrenheit	celsius	gas mark
225	105	¼
250	120	½
275	135	1
300	150	2
325	165	3
350	180	4
375	190	5
400	200	6
425	220	7
450	230	8
475	245	9

converting temperatures from an instant-read thermometer

We include doneness temperatures in many of the recipes in this book. We recommend an instant-read thermometer for the job. Refer to the table at left to convert Fahrenheit degrees to Celsius. Or, for temperatures not represented in the chart, use this simple formula:

Subtract 32 degrees from the Fahrenheit reading, then divide the result by 1.8 to find the Celsius reading. For example: "Roast chicken until thighs register 175 degrees."

To convert:
175°F − 32 = 143
143 ÷ 1.8 = 79.44°C, rounded down to 79°C

index

NOTE: Page references in *italics* indicate photographs.